CU00594942

FREE
BUT NOT EASY

narrated by
Bas Barker

written by
Lynda Straker

1989

Published by

Derbyshire County Council

I

ACKNOWLEDGEMENTS

The authors would like to acknowledge the following for supplying us with some of the photographs which appear on the pages as indicated:

Derbyshire Times: Front cover portrait, plus photographs on pages 35, 105 and 131.

Chesterfield Library: Front cover main photograph, plus photograph on page 46.

Alan Bower: Photograph on page 6, taken from his book "Chesterfield and North East Derbyshire Old Post Cards" published by Reflections of a Bygone Age.

Chesterfield Trades Council: Photograph on page 133.

All the other photographs belong to the authors.

Front Cover: Portrait of Bas Barker 1989.
Derbyshire Miners demonstrate in Chesterfield Market Place in 1902.

Back Cover: Bas, an original sketch made during Russian clown Popov's act at Moscow State Circus.

ISBN 0903463 296

DERBYSHIRE
County Council
Supports Nuclear Free Zones

Phototypeset and printed by:
Mastaprint Limited, Sandiacre, Nottingham.

THE AUTHOR

Lynda Straker

Back in the days when I was a district reporter for the Sheffield Star I came across Bas Barker who used to chair the local Community Health Council meetings. I already knew of him and had frequently watched him preside over the monthly Trades Council meetings.

But it was at the regular CHC meetings that a relationship based on respect and liking grew. I was interested in how this "Communist" was obviously able to earn the respect of both doctors and health officials on the one hand, and the workers and labour movement on the other.

When age rather than ability forced Bas to retire from the health council he was presented with a tape recorder after apparently confessing he would love to write his life story but did not know where to begin. I offered to help — and soon faced the same problem!

I expected him to be able to tell an interesting story but as I began to chart Bas' life I was amazed at the breadth of his experiences, which took him half way around the world and saw him working alongside many international figures,including the artist Picasso.

In particular I was impressed by his mental clarity and sense of humour, along with his ability to lift and inspire when things appeared to be going badly for the labour movement. I have done my best to be as inobtrusive as possible in this very modest man's life, trying always to retain his own flavour of thought and speech.

The book took longer to complete than originally anticipated for as we started in 1984 history was in the making and commitments on both our sides forced us to stop when first the Chesterfield Tony Benn By-election took place, immediately followed by the year-long miners' strike.

Bas' life spans practically the whole of the twentieth century and covers one of the most important periods in the history of the working class movement in this country.

He has dedicated practically every living breath to the labour movement and it is therefore only right that his story should lie along the same shelf as detailed accounts of the many national and international events of this period in which he played a part.

FOREWORD

by Peter Heathfield, General Secretary of the
National Union of Mineworkers

Basil Barker's autobiography graphically details the continuum of change which has taken place in the labour and trade union movement since his early involvement in the 1920s to the present date.

It shows his uncompromising determination to play a full part alongside fellow Socialists and trade unionists in the struggle to improve conditions for the mass of ordinary people in this country. In nearly 40 years of knowing Bas I have been impressed most of all by his complete dedication to the labour movement.

I first came across Bas in 1951 standing on the pump in Chesterfield Market place addressing a crowd of people. The pump was a local Speaker's Corner and Bas, I learned, was a candidate in the forthcoming parliamentary elections. As a young miner I recall being impressed by the things he was saying with an ageless charisma which he retains to this day. And, from that time onwards during my early involvement in the NUM and Labour party I was to hear many times of Bas' outstanding service to his own union, the AEU, as a leading shop steward of many years standing, and as a tireless activist within the Chesterfield Trades Council and the local political scene in the town. Little did I know then how much I would be involved alongside him and many other colleagues in wider local trade union and political activity.

His outstanding contribution in establishing the Chesterfield Trades Council May Day Demonstration, now acknowledged as one of the largest in the country, reflects this unstinting dedication to the trade union movement but also shows his great awareness of its value, not just in historical terms but also in concern for the welfare of every ordinary citizen and the future of humanity.

He is a very determined man whose personality and willingness to listen has endeared him to the broad labour movement in and outside of Chesterfield. He has never wavered from the principle that integrity motivated him and those who disagreed, and even some of his opponents, came to recognise and admire Bas as a man of great principle. This recognition was most clearly shown in 1983 when he was made a Freeman of the Borough of Chesterfield.

This factual and very human look at life of one person committed in total optimism to the cause of the labour movement has to be of great value and interest to anyone born this century.

CONTENTS

CHAPTER ONE

Earliest Memories

It was during my last years at school that I first became actively involved in politics. I have not many abiding memories of classroom life at North Wingfield and certainly cannot recall much of the academic side of lessons. But in 1922 when I was twelve I was given a task which turned out to be one of the most onerous experiences that I have ever had to undertake during the whole of my life.

Clay Cross, a small mining town to the south of Chesterfield, had by now become a separate parliamentary constituency in Derbyshire and in 1922 the Labour Party decided to put up its first candidate. There was apparently no rush in those days to become a parliamentary Labour candidate for there was little money. If a person did not have private means there was no possibility of financing a viable campaign. The man eventually chosen to represent Labour was Charles Duncan, a member of the old General Workers Union before it amalgamated and became the Municipal and General Workers Union.

By now it had become obvious to my father that of his six sons and two daughters I was the only one who shared his interest in the labour and trade union movement. And so it was agreed that, with my father's consent, I should be asked to take two days off school to help in this very important election campaign.

My job was to deliver leaflets through every door in the area and it was done during blizzards and bitterly cold conditions. It is an experience I have never forgotten and one for which I have never had to have more dedication to finish. For eight hours each day I tramped the streets delivering those leaflets. I did not dare miss out anyone for I was informed that "they" had people scattered about who would be reporting back on whether or not I had been to their door.

Such was, I suppose, my auspicious start to political life because as a result of my and other people's activities Charles Duncan became one of the country's first Labour Members of Parliament. Ever since that time I have believed that if you are intending to be sincere in what you are trying to do in politics, then it is always well to know the hum drum business of winning support rather than be — and we have a lot of them today — a prima donna who does not know the first thing about the basic activities within the movement.

I was born in Holmewood on 16th September 1910 and grew up in Grassmoor, both typical Derbyshire mining villages lying south of Chesterfield near to Clay Cross, which had all the evils and not many of the benefits of industrialisation. My mother, Eunice, used to say that Holmewood was the last place on earth that God had made, indicating that

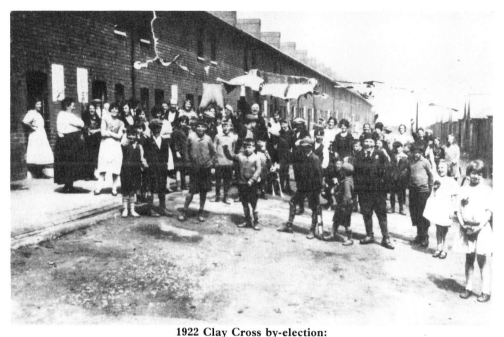

1922 Clay Cross by-election:
At 12 I was given my first political task and it turned out to be one of the most onerous.
Labour candidate Charles Duncan pictured with supporters along the town's Long Rows
(centre wearing a suit with his arm raised). The women were famous for hanging out their
enormous pairs of knickers which they wrote slogans on — see also chapter 13.

the whole place had been scraped together from the left overs of other creations. You could never say it was a bright place because the smoke, steam and grime from the colliery and coke ovens hung over the village like a dull, dark, dank smog. The houses were rows of terraces owned by the colliery and generally on unmade streets. On a dark damp day it was as grey as the life of the people who lived there.

Holmewood was created in the early days of the twentieth century to supply a labour force to the collieries and their by-product developments, and was totally dependent on the Hardwick Colliery Company.

The colliery owners and managers not only determined who should work and thereby live, but also controlled everything else in the village. They owned the pubs, colliery band, cricket and football teams and to be a member or player in any one of these largely decided what sort of job you had in the pit. For example, if you were a good cricketer and if the local pit manager was also a player and wanted you in the local team, then you were likely to get one of the better colliery jobs.

This principle was even extended to religious life for if you attended one of the non-conformist chapels, such as the Primitive Methodists or the Wesleyans, then your mode of worship was controlled by the people who ran the chapels, who were generally the colliery management or their minions. The company completed its control and bondage of miners and their families by establishing the Holmewood and Williamthorpe Co-operative Society, with the founder and first president being the colliery's managing director who proceeded to stuff the board with managers, under-managers, and deputies.

One of the most important people on the board was the treasurer, a position held through long standing tradition by the colliery manager. Through various means of intimidation and pressure, active Co-op members were advised that life and the ability to earn a living would be easier and much simpler if they did not oppose the colliery nomination. But a number of people, including my father, felt this was not a very democratic procedure and John Barker, a rebel from birth who never flinched from any decision of that sort, boldly stated that his nomination for treasurer would go forward to the annual meeting.

When the nominations had been submitted and become known the colliery management launched a campaign of intimidation and pressure demanding that the nominations be withdrawn, with all sorts of hints of what might happen to their livelihood if they did not. I remember the tense discussion at home which arose when the colliery manager warned my father that he was doing a very dangerous thing which could wreck his future as a colliery worker and advising him to withdraw. However, the nominees stood firm as the matter had now grown in to a public campaign involving the whole of the village, and at the annual meeting of the Co-op Society the colliery management resorted to the tactic of packing it with every stooge they could muster; managers, under-managers, deputies, stallmen and cronies of every sort. The result was that the new nominees were defeated by a small majority and the company maintained its hold on the Co-op Society.

In short, then, the colliery company not only owned the mines but also attempted to own and control the body and minds of the miners and their families. Men were treated as serfs and were given a job only if they accepted the company dictates.

CHAPTER TWO

Mother and Family Life

My earliest memories of life recall not merely the fact that we were poor but of the great sense of shame I felt when dressed for school or other occasions in family hand-me-downs. In fact, I can clearly remember my point blank refusal to go to school wearing a pair of shoes which had previously belonged to one of my sisters because they were what we called button-ups, shoes which were fastened by a series of buttons.

My spending money was one penny a week, less than half-a-pence in today's money, and I still recall the trauma on Friday evening or Saturday morning when I had to decide how to spend this money. This usually involved me in considerable periods of time spent glued to various local shop windows agonising over whether to plump for spending it all at once or whether to divide it in to two half-penny worths to make it last longer.

Being poor never really seemed to be something we had to be sorry about because we were kept and fed as well as my parents were able to manage. But it must have been a desperate battle constantly to feed ten of us. My mother's life of struggle and unremitting toil was a typical reflection of the life of the poor within her age. As a youngster it seemed as though she was always there early in the morning and late at night cleaning, sewing, cooking and endlessly worrying about the future. But I can never remember having to do without a meal of some sort in spite of the fact that we lived through the 1921 strike, the depression, short-time working, illness and unemployment.

Once, when my father had been off work ill with a strained heart, my mother decided to eke out the money by baking and selling cakes. She had always been an excellent cook and was a marvel with all sorts of cheap ingredients, managing to turn them into satisfying and tasty dishes. And her tea-cakes, cream cakes, Eccles cakes and bread cakes easily sold in the village. But my father, like most men of the time, believed this was something to be ashamed of because he had got in to the position where he could no longer provide the necessities of life for the family.

During the 1921 miners' dispute we had to develop eating habits that did not stretch far beyond bread and jam and the now famous potato dripping. This was a recipe which involved bones and meat fats which were bought from the butcher for a few pence and then rendered into dripping and mixed with a whole bowl of boiled potatoes, mashed together and then spread on bread. If not too appetising it certainly provided a satisfactory filling meal. Poverty of course was rife among the miners and their families at this time and most of us had the experience of leaving early for school with a mug so we could have a soup breakfast.

But the tremendous struggle of trying to keep a family of our size on a miner's wage during the disputes and battles of the early 1920s ultimately, in my view, led to my mother's early death at the age of fifty-six. When we asked the doctor what the cause was he shrugged his shoulders and said: "She was completely worn out and exhausted". Undoubtedly she gave her all for her family and like so many other miners' wives, bore the brunt of the battle throughout those long years of poverty and struggle during the early period of my life. It is a tragedy she did not live to enjoy the esteem, love and comfort of her family which she so richly deserved.

Mother was the eldest in a colourful family of twelve and therefore from an early age she had to help to bring up the younger ones in conditions of extreme poverty. Her father, Jack Cadman, was a jovial Staffordshire man who had come into Derbyshire to work as a pit sinker, an itinerant navvy-cum-miner who moved from place to place to find work wherever they were developing the new colliery.

In some cases the men stopped on and continued to work in the pit that they helped to sink, and presumably this was what Grandfather Jack did at Holmewood until he had an accident which damaged his knee. At least, this was the reason he gave ever after for not being able to work and he must have been in his forties or early fifties when he presumably decided that a further job was not conducive to his way of living.

So that was when he and Grandma Cadman decided to turn their end terraced home into a fish and chip shop, with Grandfather getting the job of peeling and chipping the potatoes. There were two rooms downstairs with two bedrooms and an attic upstairs and where they all lived and slept was a constant mystery that I for one never solved.

Grandfather's influence in the family had diminished somewhat mainly because of him not working and relying mostly on the family for his living. It was Grandmother who sat in the corner like a real matriarchial figure and ran the family, deciding what spending money she was prepared to let Grandfather have based on his previous record of not keeping rather than keeping his family. For when he was working he apparently preferred to spend his money on beer rather than his wife and children. According to my mother Grandfather was known as a hard worker, a hard drinker and a hard fighter in his younger days. He worked when he had no money but when he did have money, he spent it in the public house and showed little or no concern for the welfare of his family.

On one occasion, it seems, he was in the local public house and getting short of money so he announced that for half-a-crown (12½p) he was prepared to sell "a hen and eight chicks", and told the prospective purchaser where they could be picked up. Eventually the buyer arrived at my Grandmother's address and, telling her he had just bought a hen and eight chicks from my Grandfather, asked where they were so he could take them away. Apparently, though, this was not the first time Grandfather had sold the hen and chicks so my Grandmother was able to say: "The only hen and eight chicks that are here are me and the eight children". Grandfather had just sold his family for half-a-crown knowing, I suppose, that no purchaser would be prepared to accept the responsiblity of taking them away.

Many a time my mother told us the story of when Grandfather used to come home drunk and lay on the rug in front of the fire to sleep it off. And one of her jobs was to go stealthily through his pockets to see if she could find any money left so they could buy some food. Then, when my Grandfather regained consciousness and if he accused my Grandmother of going through his pockets, she could in all honesty declare that she had not. They relied on him being so bemused that he would not know whether he had actually had any money left.

Grandma's fish and chip shop was noted around the area and being the end house in the row Grandfather's potato peeling shack was a lean-to attached to the end row of toilets and outhouses. This provided him with a convenient vantage point from where he could exchange greetings and conduct conversations with all who passed by. It also led to him being the local doctor's "contact" man and, in his eyes at least, gave him an improved position of respect, if not authority.

Dr. Graham was the Hardwick Colliery Company doctor who was paid a capitation fee from the national insurance fund known as the "Lloyd George scheme" which covered all employed miners. But the mining areas also developed a system of medical care that became the forerunner to the National Health Service. At the Hardwick Colliery the miners negotiated with the company for a certain sum of money to be deducted each week from their wages. From these monies the company would then pay out agreed sums to the hospitals, death and accident funds and a capitation fee to the doctor to provide medical cover for the wives and children of the miners.

Hunloke Road, Holmwood — my birth place and taken around the time I was born.

6

For some reason, which I was never able to fathom, this system was called the "Field Club" and was jointly administered by the miners and the company. The company provided the clerical and administration facilities and a leading member of the company acted as nominal secretary. The miners generally provided the president or chairman, a position held by my father for many years. Through these schemes the miners were able to provide medical care for themselves, wives and families, hospital and convalescent treatment, as well as artificial limbs and, in the final extremity, grants to the next of kin in the case of fatal accidents.

Taking into consideration the time and period, these schemes were remarkable achievements of social planning and organisation and it is said that when Aneurin Bevan became Minister of Health he used the schemes that had been developed in the mining areas as the basis for planning the National Health Service. I suppose it could be said, with some justification, that it was the rough, tough conditions of life and work in the mining areas that enabled it to provide the midwife for the birth of modern social developments and legislation.

Doctor Graham therefore had the task of looking after and providing medical care for the miners, their wives and families. His main surgery was at Holmewood but he had a number of local surgeries where he hired someone's front room two days a week. If he thought you needed serious examination and attention, though, you had to visit him at Holmewood as he did not pretend to dispense serious medicine from his local surgeries.

I remember one of the rare occasions when my father was ill and the doctor paid him a visit and said he was run down and needed a tonic. Father asked if one of the children should run down to the North Wingfield surgery to pick it up, to which the doctor replied: "Good God no. I only keep coloured water there". He then explained that when a patient first complained of feeling unwell he would give them a bottle of brown coloured medicine. If on their second visit they said they had improved and were feeling better, he would repeat the dose. If they said they were no better then he changed the colour and gave them a bottle of red. The amazing thing was that it worked and everybody was happy.

Although the doctor had a number of local surgeries he did not have one at Hillyfield where my Grandparents lived. So he made arrangements with Grandfather that anyone needing the doctor should leave a message with him and these would be passed on to the doctor. Each morning on his rounds Dr. Graham would pull up opposite Grandfather's shed and, with a mixture of respect, servility and touching of the cap, Grandfather would give him the day's messages and converse on the issues of the day.

Grandfather must have been someone the doctor liked and when he discovered they shared an interest in the sport of Kings horse racing they used to have a regular discussion on the perm of the day. Grandfather always claimed he could neither read nor write so I was always puzzled at how by some fortuitous sense he could manage to decipher the names of horses listed in the racing pages to become quite an able punter. In recognition of Grandfather's services the doctor would sometimes place small bets on horses in Grandfather's name and if they won he would bring him the winnings on his next visit. These small windfalls constituted his only income so his spending money was restricted and maintaining a regular supply of tobacco for his pipe proved very difficult. But he worked out a strategy that served him well for a long time.

It was common practice in those days if you bought bread, margarine and routine groceries during the week from the local shop to put the items into what was called the shop book. You did not pay cash but when you got your wages on Friday the book was added up and the account paid, leaving you free to start buying on credit again on Monday. Grandfather often went on errands to the local shop and began to pick up the book to buy himself half an ounce of twist and a box of matches to keep his pipe going. I just happened to be present on one occasion when Grandmother was scrutinising the book and was somewhat bemused at entries put down as "½ tob. one mat." — until she discovered it was Grandfather literally doing the twist by using the book to get himself some tobacco and matches.

CHAPTER THREE

Father

I never knew much about my father's family but they must have had some special genes as they had a remarkable record of longevity. Apart from a sister who died during the influenza epidemic after the first world war, they all lived until their late eighties and early nineties, including my father.

John Barker was a face-worker at Williamthorpe Colliery and first took an interest in the trade union and political movement to try to break the strangle hold the company had over the whole of the miners' lives. His first act of defiance was when he decided to move out of the company house at Holmewood and into Highfields which, apart from being a pleasanter place to live, removed the threat of the company being able to make him homeless.

I was the fourth of eight children and we moved to 45 Highfields shortly after I was born. Presumably at that time mining was in one of its boom periods so father was able to scrape together enough money to put a deposit on a house. In those days it was regarded as being quite palatial as we had a bathroom as well as three bedrooms, which was indeed very rare. Downstairs there was a big kitchen parlour-cum-dining room and a front room. In those days in working class homes the front room was only ever used for weddings or funerals. Chair and tables legs in it used to have stockings on them to protect them from being damaged even though they were rarely used. I don't know why we should be different but my parents never did that. We ate in the kitchen but at weekends we always ate in the living room and dining room. Something in my father's make-up believed that such items were not there as show pieces but to be used to make life more enjoyable.

The atmosphere was very joyous and we were encouraged to do all sorts of things which were not in line with the normal characteristics of the day,which would now be considered part and parcel of growing up in a progressive household. For instance father introduced a rule on Sundays, which was the only full day off in a working week, when the men believed they had the right to lie in and have a day's rest. So father insisted that it was equally right to ease the burden of the women. And against the normal pattern of a Sunday in a working class household when you got up, had breakfast then immediately started preparing for dinner and tea, he decided that we could have breakfast but Sunday dinner was out and replaced by a high tea, which gave the women some time off from preparing, cooking and setting meals all day.

The house stood next to a pit branch railway line with a level crossing and signal box nearby. I remember how this signal box shone. The men who opened the gates from time to time kept the place spick and span so the brasses glittered and the floor was so clean and polished you could eat off it. One of the delights was the occasion when they allowed me and my brothers inside to sit with them, although we had to be very careful of what we did so as not to make the slightest mess.

**Mother, taken in her late teens, and father taken in his later years.
She died at 56, he lived until 90.**

My father was a self-taught man and together with his brother Alf and a number of other people they set up a reading circle. Most weekends at least one of the group would try to get to Chesterfield market and pick up a couple of books and bring them home. These were then circulated throughout the group with each member reading and passing them on after discussing the merits or the message of the book, or the quality of the writing and the author's ability. They therefore became very well educated men not only in a book learning sense but in their ability to relate to the life they lived. In view of their limited opportunities they were a remarkable group for none had had any normal schooling as we know it today.

Most had had a few years at what they called half-time school where the attendance was restricted to half a day either morning or afternoon. They had no access to libraries but they had a real love of books. For instance, even in his eighties my father could still quote extensively from the "good book" as he called it and was equally adept with Shakespeare. Another great favourite was Charles Dickens who I believe expressed their protest against the inequalities of life, and Jack London, from whose books they gained the spirit and belief that it was possible to create a movement to change society. At one time he had fifty-three volumes of which I probably now have thirty.

Such an atmosphere meant that the family was encouraged to read and were obviously aware of what was happening at the pit with its consequential affect on the village and the miners. We took the Daily Herald from its first issue and although comics were not allowed, we were encouraged to read the children's newspaper. My father played an important part in the organisation and development of activities to keep solidarity among the miners. I can remember him coming out of the pit early every Friday, for

10

which he got special concession, to stand in the pit lane for quite some time, often getting drowned with the rain, to collect trade union contributions. Eventually he moved to the luxury of a wooden hut in the pit yard.

Our family lived close to and was great friends with the Hickens and when Harry became general secretary of the Derbyshire Miners Association and moved into the official's house I spent all my weekends and holidays living with them. It was at their house where I met many of the leading figures of the labour and trade union movement and where I got my first inkling of what it all meant. In this way I was brought up within the movement and became involved in its daily discussions and fortunes picking up the flavour of political talk and activity at a relatively young age. Many is the time I have sat on the rug as a child being impressed and enthralled by the leading personalities of the movement expressing their point of view.

Harry Hicken had a phenomenal memory and a wonderful library of whole aspects connected with the general literature, history, development and activities of the labour movement. If ever you raised a question with him he would point to a book on one of the shelves and tell you to read it and find the answer. It was no good pretending you had read it because his wonderful memory enabled him to put you through a detailed interrogation of what was written. And I suppose because of his ability to remember he was a great orator. His use of language and words was something out of this world and I have no doubt that living in such an atmosphere developed in me my love of books and to always be seeking information.

It was these experiences that were later to prove invaluable to me in understanding the principles of the labour movement which were to play such an important part in my own life.

CHAPTER FOUR

Religion and the Birth of Socialism

It has been said John Wesley's service to society was to promise people pie in the sky tomorrow and thereby prevent a revolutionary situation developing in Britain, with the workers being persuaded to wait for the next world instead of fighting to improve this one. Certainly all the people in the labour movement in the mining areas who developed at this time were influenced by what was happening in the local chapels. But I am convinced from what I experienced then and have since seen that Methodism was the start of the Socialist movement and of the real militant trade unionist.

The miners used their church as an agitational forum against the social conditions of the day and preached of real Christianity and brotherhood of man, not of the Christianity based on one man or a group of people exploiting another, which was the formal establishment religion as experienced through the Church of England. Many of the leading trade union figures who grew up in those days developed from lay preachers in Methodist chapels throughout the area. Most were said and believed to be the wonder preachers of their day, using the pulpit as the means to get across the message of Socialist Christianity which was their creed.

They would attack every social evil, such as the actions of the colliery managers and coal bosses, poverty and low wages or the evils of the tied housing system, while at the same time arguing for more cultural activities for workers across the whole breadth of society. All this was done, of course, through hymns mainly based on the Sankey hymn book which provided them with the means to sing of their ideals, with "God When Wilt Thou Save The People" becoming a near anthem in the Methodist chapels of that day.

But in Holmewood the colliery management and its stooges had already taken over the administration machine of the chapel and ran it in the interests of the company. So if the miners were to have a chapel in which they could preach the gospel according to their own ideals and under their own control, they would have to start one of their own. And so the Lings Row Chapel was born.

My father became deeply involved in the chapel's development and I feel sure the enthusiasm, energy, tenacity and sacrifice put into building the chapel was not just extended in the hope of providing a niche for themselves in the hereafter, but rather in an expressed desire for a place where they believed they could discuss the future and have some say in improving the present. The chapels became the social centres of the villages with people organising organ recitals, religious performances and reading recitals. I remember the enthusiasm, tension and expectation when such people as Harrison Ainsworth, who was regarded as a great elocutionist, came to give an evening of Dickens recitals. The chapels became a scene of cultural development where people could escape from the dread and poverty-stricken reality of life.

Prayer meetings were a real free-for-all and as a young child I remember the adults getting up and realistically expressing their thoughts. In particular I have an abiding memory of an old man with white hair and a flowing white beard called Mr. Hunt who brought all the fears of damnation and final trepidation to anyone who had transgressed in the slightest way. He could put the fear of God into me by making me believe that every small transgression I made, be it a white lie or failing to clean my shoes, would be sure to be condemned by old man Hunt. His power of prayer, though, was subsequently weakened when it was discovered that as a widower he had acted as a human being with a married lady, much to the annoyance of her husband!

When I asked my father some years later why it was that he and others eventually became disillusioned with the chapels as a way of advancing the well being of the working people, he said it happened during the first world war. All the chapels, churches and the establishment were urging people to pray for a victory for our armed forces, and the Germans were equally calling on the Lord to give them victory. It was then, he said, that he realised the Lord had a fearful job on trying to give victory to both sides and so there had to be something wrong with a theory of that kind.

So he left Methodisim and devoted his activities to the development of the Socialist movement through the trade union and Labour party.

CHAPTER FIVE

1924 Chesterfield Parliamentary Elections

The year we moved to Grassmoor, which lay in the Chesterfield constituency, coincided with the two 1924 parliamentary elections, the first of which succeeded in establishing the first minority Labour government.

In Chesterfield it was the first time there had been a specific Labour party candidate contesting the seat. Prior to then it was held by what was euphemistically called the Lib-Labs in the form of Barnett Kenyon, an official of the Derbyshire miners who pledged his allegiance to the Liberal party. Up until then it had been agreed that it was unnecessary for the unions to ally themselves to one of the leading political parties to enable them to influence the appropriate legislation that was tabled in parliament.

Barnett Kenyon was an old man who complained bitterly during the election campaign that by putting up their own candidate, Labour and the Derbyshire miners were acting like traitors who wanted to see a poor old man lose his living. I was only a kid at the time but I attended some of the election meetings and to see him performing on the platform, doing his poverty-stricken act, had to be seen to be believed. It was more like one of the old-time music hall acts than real serious politics.

Throughout the previous two years Chesterfield constituency party had been discussing the possibility of adopting a parliamentary candidate and had contacted and interviewed a number of people, but had had little success in persuading anyone to contest the seat until Hugh Dalton — who eventually became Chancellor of the Exchequer in the Labour government — agreed to become a candidate. Preparations were made to hold an adoption meeting and introduce him to the members but at the last minute he declined the invitation. This was in 1923 and there was already an air of expectancy of an early general election. So, after many disappointments, the local party decided to ask its national headquarters to suggest a candidate.

They came up with George Benson, a Manchester estate agent whose father had been a supporter and treasurer of the Independent Labour Party. According to the local minutes, while there was neither an overwhelming nor universal support for his candidature, the fact that he had been a conscientious objector during the first world war and had been imprisoned for his beliefs, which were in line with local party feeling, tipped the scales in his favour. In later years, of course, it was proved that George Benson was no militant.

Obviously the other two parties made the running because this was a new venture as far as the labour movement was concerned. But we delivered the leaflets, did our canvassing and at the end of the day, collected 6,303 votes. The election result nationally led to a minority Labour government being formed under Ramsay MacDonald which lasted for just nine months.

Within the local labour movement there was a general feeling of excitement and expectation with the break through of having achieved the first Labour government, but it achieved little to improve the life of the working people. Already MacDonald and company were mouthing the cliche: "We are only in office, not in power". There was an uneasy parliamentary alliance between Labour and the Liberals, who eventually joined with the Tories in bringing down the government on the issue of the Campbell case.

J.R. Campbell, who I subsequently came to know very well, was at the time editor of the Workers Weekly and was arrested and charged under the 1797 Incitement to Mutiny Act for publishing an article urging soldiers not to fire on strikers or civilian workers in an industrial dispute. The labour movement and Labour MPs protested to the government and, in the face of a storm of protest, it offered no evidence in court against Campbell and dropped the case. The Tories, Liberals, press and establishment developed an anti-communist and anti-Soviet scare and eventually turned out the Labour government, helped by the notorous Zinoviev letter.

This was a letter purporting to be instructions from Moscow to the British Communist Party on how to bring down the British government by way of revolution. It was immediately declared to be a forgery by those who were supposed to have received it and was later proved beyond any shadow of a doubt to be so. But it nevertheless did the trick of helping the Tories win the October 1924 general election.

In Chesterfield George Benson was once again the Labour candidate and Barnett Kenyon, the sitting MP, was opposing him. By this time Kenyon, who had retained his position as agent for the Derbyshire miners while an MP, had been relieved of his duties as a union official for constantly attacking union policy and not attending council meetings.

He was given a £2 weekly pension and allowed to keep the tenancy of a union house, but he combined stories of being thrust into poverty because of his efforts on behalf of the miners and having to live on bread and cheese with real tears running down his cheeks to emphasise his humility and sacrifice.

In truth he was an old humbug who the miners treated better than he deserved. But it was a real virtuoso performance and certainly won him votes with him holding his seat by 13,971 votes to George Benson's 9,206. At the count I remember George declaring: "At the last election we polled 6,000 votes. This time we have turned the six upside down and next time we shall turn Chesterfield upside down".

And this he did for at the next election in 1929 George Benson became Chesterfield's first Labour member of Parliament and the Labour movement believed it had finally arrived.

CHAPTER SIX

Politics leading up to the General Strike

It should be understood that the development of the labour movement in Britain is peculiar to our British conditions. There is no socialist movement or party on the continent or elsewhere that has developed on the same basis as the one in Britain. The British labour movement, particularly the Labour party, grew up out of a federation of trade unions, socialist societies, the Independent labour party and Fabian society and a number of other organisations that came together in the initial 1906 Representation Committee.

It is because of this development on a federal basis that the British labour movement was able to combine the various strands and strata throughout the movement. It should always be remembered that a large number of the so-called leaders of today could never have been leaders of the Labour party until the rules had changed. For up to 1918 you could not be an individual member of the Labour party. Individual members with socialist ideals were catered for within the ILP and other members of the Labour party were members based on their membership of the trade unions or the various sections and strands that all came together under the Labour Representation Committee to form the Labour party, which ran candidates from 1906 onwards.

Because of how it developed it was possible for all sides of the movement to hammer out together a collective policy which all then could at least support. Not until the 1924 Labour party conference did you see the base of the Labour party's membership narrow and develop, a decision in my view which is probably responsible for the large amount of disunity that has developed throughout the labour movement in Britain to this day. As one who has spent a lifetime in the movement it always seemed to me that one of the more tragic occurrences came at the 1924 Liverpool Labour party conference when the Communists were expelled from membership and we had the beginning of the introduction of the Black Circulars, which proscribed members of certain organisations from being members of the Labour party.

The Chesterfield Communist Party was formed by a small group of people around 1926 when I would be about sixteen. Because of my age I would ordinarily have had to belong to the Young Communist League, but due to the fact that I was the only one and they didn't have any Young Communist League cards I was given a CP card. So I joined the Communist party as a founder member of the Chesterfield CP and I have had a CP card ever since.

In those days there was not the bitterness, segregation and ostracization as there is today generally with the Left. There was a general agreement that you were adhering to some sort of principles which were commonly expressed and that we were all after the same thing, it was just that we were going about it in a different sort of way. The fact that I was speaking on Labour party platforms in 1931 proved that we were accepted as part of the labour movement.

Even though MacDonald and his cohorts produced what eventually became the Black Circulars, it was not always applied in the localities and in Chesterfield was not applied with any precision or determination. So while I held a CP card in 1931 I was also on the Labour party executive because nobody objected to that. If you were prepared to work for the movement and applied yourself to the principles of the advancement of the working class, you were accepted. There were no questions raised in relation to your attitudes and you had your separate meetings and contributed to the wider general meetings of the Constituency Labour Party on that basis.

Since the end of the first world war the Tories had been trying to defeat and remove any of the privileges or advances that the working class had made as a result of the war. They were anxious again to rest their supremacy both in business at home and abroad and over the working class forces. So this was a time of real political fermentation. The workers were attempting to fight back with a coal strike in 1921, an engineers' lock-out a year later and various battles within both transport and the railways.

Therefore, by 1924 these political problems were becoming more sharpened in their intensity and with the return of the Tory government after the defeat of the Labour minority government there was also tremendous discussion going on within the Labour movement itself - the familar battle of the left arguing for more militant and progressive policies against the right wing, led by Ramsay MacDonald, P. Snowden, J.R. Clynes, Thomas and the rest.

As discussions went on within the movement on what particular policy and what steps should be taken to defend itself, a minority more militant organisation was set up within the trade union and labour movement, led by Harry Pollitt, and which existed to put forward progressive policies to deal with the immediate situation inside the movement at that time. By now it was early 1925 and the mine owners were saying that come July they would demand a reduction in wages and a lengthening of the working day.

Now in those days probably the two best organised groups either of the ruling class or the working class were, on the one hand the mine owners and, on the other hand the miners. There were more than a million miners in Britain making it the biggest single industry in the country. The mine owners were demanding that due to their inability, or so they claimed, to export coal profitably to build up their trade, they needed cuts in wages to help solve the economic crisis in which Britain had found itself. So the campaign, which ultimately ended with the battle of the General Strike, started.

As the discussions continued on both sides the miners, transport workers and railwaymen decided to form a pact which history now knows as the Red Friday Triple Alliance. The agreement was that if the coal owners insisted on reducing wages and lengthening hours then an embargo would be put on coal to back the miners. The Tory government, obviously not yet ready for their show-down, decided to intervene and promised the coal owners a subsidy on each ton of coal raised for nine months to allow discussions to take place between the owners and the miners. I don't think anyone now believes that the Tories and Stanley Baldwin had any intention of trying to find a solution during the course of the following nine months. But they knew that during that time they could set up their own organisation and prepare for battle when the time came. Indeed, it is said that Winston Churchill was one of the hawks who wanted to declare battle straight away but was persuaded that they would have a better chance of conducting the battle in nine months time.

The Triple Alliance's decision in 1925 to back the miners has always been referred to as Red Friday, signifying a victory for the united forces of the working class and trade union movement. And it was about a week later when Vin Williams, a leading rank and file Derbyshire miner, organised a tremendous demonstration at Renishaw Park, the seat of the well known literary Sitwells, but who also had their wealth based on coal and who lived at Renishaw Hall between Chesterfield and Sheffield.

Now Vin, who always had flair and vision, believed a big demonstration was necessary to mobilise the working class for the battle ahead. Renishaw Hall and Renishaw Park looked to him to be an ideal setting and when someone asked him how he thought he was going to get permission to use the park — because the Sitwells were not noted as supporters of the labour movement — Vin's simple reply was, "We'll go up to the door and ask". And that was exactly what he did. He marched through the park up to the door, rang the bell and, in his words, "a flunky appeared and opened the door". He looked very distressed and disdainful when he saw Vin at the door but Vin, not dismayed, asked: "Is S'roswald in?" The butler, or whoever was opening the door, was inclined to turn Vin away, but he could not have known Vin who insisted on seeing Sir Oswald Sitwell to outline his plans for this demonstration. And he got his permission to use the park.

All the trade union movement over a very wide area was circulated with details and on that particular Saturday one of the largest demonstrations of a political nature that ever took place in Derbyshire was held at Renishaw Park. Vin had arranged for most of the speakers to call for lunch at Harry Hickens' before going on to the demonstration. And I remember as a lad being amongst a great collection of speakers, such as A.J. Cooke and Herbert Smith, general secretary and president respectively of the Miners' Federation, Oliver Baldwin, Stanley Baldwin's son who was also a Labour party member and candidate, and Malcolm MacDonald, a Labour party candidate for Bassetlaw and Ramsay MacDonald's son, as well as two other then prominent members of the Labour party, Sir Oswald and Lady Cynthia Mosley. And even now I recall the warnings of A.J. Cooke that inspite of our enthusiasm about the victory which had been achieved on Red Friday, it was only the beginning. The whole of the labour movement, he said, had to start preparing for the next round in the battle which he believed would take place in May the following year when the government's coal subsidy ran out.

That warning was a prophetic one. Unfortunately nobody listened or, if they did, they hadn't the will to make the necessary preparations to win the next battle, which did come the following year.

CHAPTER SEVEN

The General Strike

I was sixteen and unemployed when the miners were locked out and the General Strike took place. My father was intimately connected with the mining industry and as a delegate and member of the Derbyshire Miners Association executive was particularly involved in the various discussions and activities surrounding the problem of what was to happen when the government's subsidy to the coal owners ran out. It was clear the miners had made up their minds that, rather than submit to the coal owners' proposals to slash wages and increase their hours of work, they would fight back.

However, in spite of their determination to resist these attacks on their standard of living, as the months rolled by there was no great feeling or preparation either locally or nationally by the trade union movement to meet what was obviously going to be a new situation. So when the General Strike did come there was a great amount of relief among the miners that trade union support was being given to them even though few had prepared for the situation.

The miners, it is said, were not involved in the strike. They were locked out. The coal owners had indicated to the miners and their Federation and their various district organisations that if at the end of April they were not prepared to work under the new proposals then the pits would close and they would be locked out. In fact the miners finished work on the Friday prior to May 1st while the General Strike did not start until May 3rd 1926. The miners held meetings in halls, chapels, pubs, club rooms and, in good weather, on open pieces of spare ground all over the area. They involved leading pit and local officials and were very well attended, so I imagine that of all the people who did understand the situation it was the miners themselves.

Indeed their understanding and preparedness to fight was underlined in the activities which immediately took place in mining areas. For as soon as the lock out was a fact of life the miners in the localities immediately started organising collection funds to set up food kitchens as part of their all-out battle in defence of their own conditions. I am bound to say that if there had been the same sort of spirit and determination to win among the leadership of the trade union movement then there would have been no doubt that the whole history of our movement, and probably the country, would have changed. But that was not to be.

In Chesterfield the General Strike committee was set up under the auspices of the Trades Council. It met in the then new Miners' Welfare at Chester Street and from where all the strike activities were directed. The committee was largely composed of miners' representatives, although there was a broad section of other trade unions involved including printers and railway people. One of the committee's jobs was to authorise permits to allow food and essential commodities to be transported to hospitals and other essential services. The pickets were on the main roads leading into the town and lorries were stopped and asked where they were going. If they had not got a permit and the pickets were satisfied that they were essential deliveries then they were sent to the miners' welfare to get a permit.

During the general strike Vin Williams was arrested for sedition and issuing statements likely to cause a breach of the peace. His 'crime' was to re-print a statement published in some of the other news sheets reporting that some army regiment of soldiers had refused to take action against some of the strikers, and Vin added that this proved blood was thicker than water and that the soldiers and the working class in the armed forces were not prepared to turn against their brothers involved in the strike who were fighting for reasonable wages and conditions.

So he was arrested, fined £5 and sent to jail for two months. Curiously the Chairman of the magistrates bench which fined him was Harry Cropper, leader of the Labour group on Chesterfield town council. And I remember hearing him justify the fact that he had to inflict this punishment on Vin because he was the chief magistrate and he had to abide by the direction of the clerk of the court. But he was also on the emergency committee which had been established by the government to maintain essential services during the course of the strike.

When the police came to arrest Vin they also raided the central strike headquarters at the miners' welfare. Presumably they were looking for documents to try to add to the charge and to try to make out that the strike committee was responsible for issuing these seditious statements. But while they were discussing searching the premises for documents Ann Astwood, a member of the strike committee and a member of the ILP connected with the early labour movement, grabbed the minute book — which contained all the names of those on the committee — and other important documents and stuffed them down the front of her dress so the police couldn't find them.

And it was significant that they did not get hold of the minutes because at a later stage the local Derbyshire Times newspaper issued summonses against the people they thought were members of the strike committee after they called for people to boycott the paper because it was being produced by blackleg labour. But the paper had to eventually withdraw the charges because as it did not actually have a list of the members of the committee, it ended up issuing summonses to all sorts of people who had no connections whatsoever with the committee. So Annie not only saved the minutes but also the members of the committee.

Vin's arrest meant the Chesterfield strike news sheet lasted for less than a week. It was sold at a halfpenny a copy, as was commonly done throughout the country, and consisted of a single sheet of paper, duplicated on both sides, which was the only way we had of passing on information on the strike as not many people in those days had radios. So they were really important organisational material to have and they appeared either daily or on alternative days. In Sheffield the strike committee ended up producing their news sheet from one of George Fletchers bread vans because the police were trying to track down and confiscate the printing machinery. So the typewriter and duplicator was moved to a bread van and became instantly mobile and undetectable.

The General Strike lasted just nine days in spite of tremendous solidarity throughout the area. I remember seeing a minute recorded by the secretary of the strike committee, Dennis Webster, which says that when they first got the news that the General Strike had ended they just couldn't believe it. Ultimately they had to believe it but they were so frustrated and angry that they recorded that the situation among the strikers and trade unions was more solid at the end than it was at the beginning, and all those on the committee and associated with it "felt a great sense of betrayal".

CHAPTER EIGHT

1926 The Miners' Strike

The end of the General Strike left the miners completely isolated to continue the long and bitter battle on their own. There was a real bitterness amongst the mining fraternity, even in my own family, that they had been betrayed. They felt that if the Trades Union General Council and the rest of the movement had had the political will if nothing else, then at least the miners could have been saved from the tremendous battle that they were about to encounter.

As the dispute developed there was a gradual return to work in some areas and mass pickets were mounted at various pits in which the women played an important part. It is probably true to say that when it came to shouting "blackleg" and such, then the women were even more vocal than the men because obviously they were having to bear the brunt of the burden of trying to provide for even the basic necessities of life. The miners' strike fund, never adequate, soon ran out so there was real poverty and it's a wonder how people managed.

Soup kitchens were set up for school children but other than that there was nothing but the Public Assistance Board which gave out vouchers for food up to a certain value. This was then charged against an individual who had to sign a document to say he would repay the loan once he returned to work, and some of the miners were having stoppages from their wages for years after to repay their debt to the Board.

With the mass picketing came the police from Manchester who were brought into Chesterfield and the surrounding area because they presumably felt that members of the local police would have some sympathy with the miners as many were recruited from local working class and mining families. But there were many complaints of viciousness and intimidation by the Manchester police, particularly against the women.

During the miners lock out there were a number of meetings held throughout the area involving leading national figures. A.J. Cooke addressed a meeting in Tapton Park and another at Tibshelf as general secretary of the Miners Federation. He was a remarkable man who was literally destroyed during and after the strike because his campaign to attempt to win the battle extracted a tremendous sacrifice in his health. Cooke fought to the full extent of his strength but the fact that he was isolated and vilified by the press, and eventually by the people in the labour movement itself, took a toll on his health and he eventually developed cancer in his leg and ended up having to have both legs amputated. He was a tragic figure of the movement, a hero amongst the miners in the sense that he was the only representative who miners believed was fulfilling the task as a leader, but caught in a battle which undoubtedly isolated and destroyed him, leading to his death in the early 1930s as a comparatively young man.

Many of the meetings were broken up by the police with speakers being arrested and charged with spreading sedition, including James Maxton, chairman of the ILP. I recall one particular Communist party meeting which I chaired at the back of the old Clay Cross Hippodrome which now no long exists. We used the back fire escape as a platform and got Clarence Mason, a shop assistant who worked for Ormes at Bakewell, to speak. We were about half-way through the meeting when a police car arrived and arrested Clarence and charged him with sedition likely to cause a breach of the peace. The next morning he appeared in court and was released on bail after Sam Sales, vice-president of the Derbyshire Miners Association, agreed to stand bail. When the case came to court at Derby a local solicitor called Smith suddenly appeared and offered to defend him on the basis that he supported the miners and was sympathetic to their point of view. But Clarence still got sent to jail for two months and, of course, lost his job with Ormes.

As the months dragged on it gradually became clear that Nottinghamshire and Derbyshire were the weak links in the miners' organisation. In the Nottinghamshire coalfield Spencerism developed, a breakaway movement led by one of the leaders of the Nottinghamshire miners who argued for separate agreements and for the miners to go back to work on the basis of negotiating separate district agreements.

Apart from being an agent of the coal miners, Spencer was also knowledgeable about Nottinghamshire which meant that because Nottinghamshire was a geologically favourable area, miners had got thick coal seams and better conditions than anywhere else to mine in. He felt that on that basis he could negotiate favourable terms for the people in that area, and certainly the coal owners gave him their fullest support. His campaign was based on a union which would only be concerned with the miners and not the politics or be connected with the labour movement in any way, and it spread into a number of Derbyshire area pits. Even today Bolsover and Creswell collieries, geographically in Derbyshire, remain part of the Nottinghamshire mining area because when the National Union of Mineworkers was formed from the old Federation it was agreed that all the pits within each district's organisation should be retained in that area.

The strike or 'lock out' was eventually called off in the November, seven months after it began. And eventually a large number of people were victimised, including my own father. When he went back to his old pit after the end of the dispute they refused to employ him. My father told the manager he could not understand why he was prepared to let blacklegs work rather than people who had been helping in the strike, because he said if a blackleg was so unprincipled as to betray his own fellow men then there was no doubt he would certainly be prepared to betray an employer.

The following March the colliery manager sent his chauffeur in the company car to our home. He came to the door and told my father that the manager wanted to see him and had sent the car to take him to the pit. My father turned around and said: "Well you go back and tell him I will come and see him but I'm walking because if he's offering to give me anything like a ride then he'll want sommat back for it, and I'm not prepared to be put in that position. I'll come, but I'm walking". And he did.

CHAPTER NINE

1929 and 1931 Parliamentary Elections

After the General Strike and the defeat of the miners the trade union movement was at a particularly low ebb. The government decided to take its revenge with the introduction in 1927 of Sir John Simon's anti-trade union laws which restricted picketting, and the introduction of the contracting-in principle for members of the trade union movement, as against the method of contracting out, for paying political levies. And this continued until 1945 when the Labour government repealed it after regaining power following the second world war.

Before the General Strike Baldwin had said that not only miners but everyone else had to suffer a reduction in the standard of living, and he declared that the wages of all workers must come down. This anti-trade union attitude of the government was further developed with the introduction of the Mond-Turner rationalisation proposals. Sir Alfred Mond, who was Chairman of ICI, and Ben Turner, who later became a Sir, got together to launch a campaign which they called Peace in Industry in which the employers on the one side, and the trade union movement on the other, would get together to solve the problems in a peaceful manner without having to resort to industrial strife and activity of that sort.

Rationalisation was a new word for that time. It was merely a term for creating unemployment. They closed down ship yards while factories transferred their order books so that unemployment eventually rose from one-and-a-half million to nearly three million by the time the '30s arrived. It was all done on the basis that it was necessary to find a new way instead of the trade union movement developing and organising its forces. Peaceful discussions with the employers really meant the worker should be prepared to accept what the employers wished to impose on them and to do it in a spirit of co-operation. In other words, it was the workers making the sacrifices to give up their wages and accept a reduced standard of living to the glory of the employers profits — not much different from what was to be argued 50 years later in the 1980s under Thatcher.

It spread a blight on the whole of the working class movement whose morale was at its lowest depths. Conferences and meetings were held in opposition to the anti-trade union bill and I became a joint secretary, along with Harry Hicken, in organising the campaign to try to stop the Bill. But we failed to spark off any great activity and ultimately the Bill became law. Only with the eventual coming of the 1929 election did the labour movement seem to recover some of its spirit.

In Chesterfield the election was viewed as an opportunity eventually to get a Labour candidate elected. The whole campaign was a particularly exhilarating experience because there was real enthusiasm and very big meetings held throughout the constituency. Our candidate was once again

George Benson, but I particularly remember his election agent John Henry Harvey who was the son of the Harvey whose statue stands in front of the Derbyshire Miners Chesterfield offices on Saltergate.

John Harvey was a wonderful Walter Mitty. He could tell endless tales, most of which were the result of his own fantasising rather than anything to do with fact. He had been in the movement for some time and was secretary of the Chesterfield Constituency Labour party for quite a period in the '20s and was presumably the only figure who had any knowledge of running an election campaign, particularly when it came to the technical details. The first Labour Party headquarters ever established in Chesterfield had just been set up at an old club room attached to the Free Mason Arms at the bottom of Newbold Road and Harvey was paid an honorarium for his work as election agent. Suddenly, in the middle of the campaign, he decided he wasn't being paid enough for his services and demanded his honorarium be doubled or he would resign. There was a crisis meeting of the executive committee and ultimately George Benson decided he would put up the extra money Harvey was demanding.

There was euphoria among the Chesterfield labour movement when George Benson was declared the winner and became the town's first Labour Member of Parliament, while Ramsay MacDonald was able to form another Labour minority government. But it soon withered when the activists began to realise there was no real socialist intent to the government's actions.

The crisis came to a head in '31 when MacDonald, Thomas, Snowden and Sankey split the labour movement by forming the first National government with Stanley Baldwin. The labour movement was depressed and dispirited when the National government went to the country for the '31 elections.

The row centred mainly on the argument that it was necessary to cut public expenditure by reducing wages by 10 per cent, including those on unemployment and social benefits and in the armed forces. This action prompted what is now known in history as the Invergordon Revolt when the sailors of the Atlantic Fleet refused to sail until their 10 per cent cut in wages was restored. It was the first revolt in the British Navy since 1797 and their victory no doubt led to the call for a general election.

It is my belief that the attitude and treachery of MacDonald and company didn't merely lose the labour movement the chance to be in government but had a fundamental effect on it for many, many years. Everybody had to try and justify the attitudes and principles of these people, who continued to live in a wealth of luxury as a result of their treachery. It had a tremendous effect on the movement, as activists were forced to question who they could trust and how they could persuade people to believe in the labour movement when at the first crunch or decisive battle with opposing forces they merely ran and joined them.

Benson hadn't a great deal of fundamental criticism of MacDonald and tended to argue that if Labour could only be given another chance their moderation would see the country through the crisis. I had already started on public speaking and spoke at various election meetings, one of which I now recall with wry amusement.

In those days it was quite common for a candidate to have two or three meetings in a night, so he started at one place and moved on to another before it ended. On this particular occasion Benson was to speak at Barlow — hardly the hot bed of revolution — then move on, and I was to follow and wind up the meeting. Benson made his speech and then left me to follow, still proclaiming the virtues and benefits of full-blown socialism. Afterwards I was trying to find a means of getting back to Chesterfield when someone suggested I took the pit bus, which was a little like a hen coop on wheels.

So this small van with seats in turned up with a small light barely illuminating the inside. I sat at the back in the dark and as the miners got on they were asking each other if they had been to the meeting. Some had, some had not but when someone was asked what it had been like I recall him replying: "Well, there's been a youngster there and I think he will have lost Benson more votes that he got him". That made me crouch back in the corner and refuse to declare myself, keeping silent all the way back to Chesterfield. But the incident always reminds me that although you may think you are doing well your audience may think completely differently. The miner on the bus had obviously been taken aback by what would today be called an extreme speech. I've always remembered the experience and it's true to say I never told George Benson about it.

The Tory candidate in Chesterfield had previously been the Marquis of Hartington or someone from the Devonshire family, but on this this occasion they put up R.J. Conant, a county farmer squire-type who obviously had no knowledge of politics or anything else. It was said that during the campaign his longest speech was of just five minutes duration and that the only speech he subsequently made in the House of Commons was to ask someone to shut the door.

Benson's agent this time was P.H. Raynes, a pottery worker and member of the Labour party who eventually became chairman of the Chesterfield Co-operative Society. Because of John Harvey's behaviour during the '29 campaign Benson decided he could no longer do business with him and so chose a new agent. Harvey always claimed it was because Labour changed its agent that it lost the election, which upset Raynes so we had to assure him that he was not the only cause as MacDonald and company had played a major role.

Nevertheless, losing the seat created a feeling of real despondency amongst the activists and the whole effect of winning in '29 was quickly dissipated.

CHAPTER TEN

Education

The desire for education and striving to become articulate seemed particularly strong among the miners. I left school at fourteen and have not many abiding memories about my days at North Wingfield school, and certainly do not recall much about the academic side of life. Among those who stand out in my mind was an old teacher called Mr. Mottershaw who seemed to believe the education of his Standard Two class was incomplete if his students had not memorised by heart the poem "Play up and play the game", allying life to cricket. The most popular teacher was probably Mr. Barlow who at least treated you as a person and was responsible for eastablishing a school football team. The school also had an allotment close by and gardening became part of the curriculum for the older students. And I can still remember the astonishment and pride of being declared one of the winners in the annual gardening competition. I didn't believe it possible then that my gardening powers were such as to be able to win prizes and I certainly don't believe they have improved any since.

My first real introduction to books came through my father's reading circle where I became a life-long admirer of Jack London and Charles Dickens. As a teenager I became connected to a group of miners at North Wingfield. These miners — the Gascoynes, Buck Hartshorn, Sam Hart and others — all attempted an adult education course organised by the Oxford University tutorial classes. This organisation was similar to the Workers Education Association but had at the same time some direct connection with Oxford University. Its aim, as with the WEA, was to provide educational facilities and opportunities for the workers but, as again with the WEA, the students who attended the classes were mainly white collar and middle class. Manual workers were rare birds indeed.

Therefore the North Wingfield class for the organisation was a real jewel indeed; a class of real miners, highly intelligent and articulate. The subjects covered were varied and we had lectures on economics, literature and politics to name but a few. I was taken in by the older miners as a student to be given help and guidance and it proved invaluable to me during the rest of my life. Subjects were discussed in down to earth style and in relation to life itself. They had no time for the abstract as life was too serious, too grim, too real for them to play about.

One course in particular that I remember studying was Aristotle's Politics and Plato's Republic. The tutor had been waxing lyrically at great length about the development of democracy in ancient Greece, where the elders gathered in the market place to argue and refine the ultimate truth. This, he said, was democracy where decisions were based on knowledge and argument.

When it came to discussion time Buck Hartshorn leaned his head on one side and tilted his squint eye upwards. Buck was one of those amazing characters who was a fiend for knowledge. He was quiet and unassuming but read widely and stored what he read. He never wore a collar and tie, always preferring a silk neckerchief and his flat cap indoors or out. And he had the amazing ability of being able to puncture the greatest windbag with a shrewd couple of sentences which would carry profound wisdom. Buck turned to the lecturer and said: "I've listened with great interest but there is one thing which puzzles me". "Oh", said the tutor, "and what is that Mr. Hartshorn?" "Well," said Buck, "I can understand very well about all this discussion going on in the market place and searching for the ultimate truth, but what I want to know is while all these bods were in the market place doing all the talking and discussing, who was doing the work?" Buck had asked the classical question. Because the development of the so called Greek democratic state was undoubtedly based on their ability to use slave labour and, for the slaves, democracy or freedom did not exist.

The miners on this course gave me great help and encouragement. They recommended books to read and widened my literary horizons considerably and persuaded me to apply for a two week summer school scholarship at Oxford university. To qualify I had to write a 300 to 400 word essay and fill in an application form. Imagine how I felt, learning that I had been successful. A fortnight at Balliol college with its facilities all placed at my disposal and the use of college quarters that would be occupied in the normal session by the regular students. Board and lodgings were completely free but I still had to find seventeen shillings (85 pence) for my fare. As I was unemployed this was not an easy task especially as the Labour exchange took the decision that I would not be able to draw benefit while away as I would not, they said, be available for work.

Oxford was a new world to those of us who came from working class backgrounds. This was the period when the means test was being viciously applied and to be unemployed in the '30s meant that you were very poor and in poverty, and those who administered the social benefits ensured it was so. Going to Balliol was like moving out of one world into another. The working class students marvelled at the atmosphere and surroundings, the comfort and facilities — and the food. Meals back home that you only ever dreamed of became every meal we ate. It was a situation that was akin to paradise as against the realities of life back home and it made me comment that anyone who could not study in those circumstances must be a dull head indeed.

Then you realised that this was something that other people regarded as their norm, which illustrated the great gap between the living standards of those that had and those that had not, and made me wish we could proceed with our general policies, attitudes and organisation so that these sort of privileges would no longer be the property and prerogative of the few. The rooms I was allocated were used in normal term times by Lord Burghley who eventually became the Olympic hurdler. I did not meet him but he left a note in the rooms welcoming whoever the student might be, with his hopes and good wishes for a pleasant stay. In fact it was a very happy time and I ended up staying twice as long as originally planned. The WEA Oxford tutorial organisation took over the college for a month in total, running two schools of a fortnight each.

During the course of lectures and discussions I made myself heard, and I suppose because of my participation I was invited by some of the tutors to stay on for a second fortnight and give a couple of lectures on a worker looking at literature. Being unemployed there was nothing to draw me back home but I was desperately short of money because of the problem of signing on. But the tutors provided me with such pocket money as to make it one of my most affluent periods, and I have an inkling that they raised it amongst themselves. The extended stay at Balliol proved a salutory lesson for me because it made me aware that if you are going to make declarations then you have got to be sure of your facts, be able to back up your point of view and always make careful preparations before making public pronouncements. This was one of the real lessons that I was taught by my visit to this awesome seat of learning in Oxford.

It was about this time, after the '31 election and during one of my short-time working periods at the colliery, that I decided to apply for a Miners Welfare scholarship. This was available to people who worked in or about the mines or their sons and daughters and was at Nottingham University for two days a week. I got it and ended up going to Nottingham every Monday and Tuesday for two years and being paid to go to college was a godsend. Our subjects were economics, economic history, industrial history and logic, which we thoroughly enjoyed, with the exception of logic.

I remember having a history tutor who claimed to be the brother of Miriam in D.H. Laurence's Sons and Lovers, while my fellow students included Les Ellis, who eventually became a full-time official of the Nottinghamshire Miners Union, Bernard Taylor who is now Lord Taylor of Mansfield, and a young man whose name escapes me but who asked me to help him with his spare time job. This involved going to the library and writing a sermon for a small organisation that supplied them to vicars and parsons. He used to get half-a-crown for each sermon, and for my help in writing them he used to pass on a modest rake off of this money. It still tickles me to think of these vicars reading out their sermons little realising they had been written by an ex-chapel goer and Communist party member! Another of the students in our group was a remarkable man who was unemployed but who had previously been playing in the Bournemouth municipal orchestra and who had a wide knowledge of all sorts of things, while another ended up as a professor teaching at Hull university.

So these were interesting and very happy times. Nowadays, even in working class education, the whole aim of education appears to be to get a job somewhere at the end of it all. Obviously there were some on our course looking for better prospects but for Les, myself and most others we wanted to get educated for our own self esteem and knowledge, so we would be more able to argue the cause in support of the working class movement generally. They sometimes say nowadays, only become educated on the basis of self return. But the fact I did all these things enabled me to have a much broader vision and view which was so valuable and which I believe education is all about. The fact that I have been able to work with and move about with books and music provided me with a much better insight than if I had not had the benefit of these things. They used to argue — and some still do it today — that it was useless to educate daughters because girls grew up only to attract a husband and then settled back as a wife and mother. They had no conception of education being of value in itself. The fact is people, whoever they are, are much better off the more knowledge they have of the world. It is something I believe all adult education should aim for.

CHAPTER ELEVEN

Unemployment and the NUWM Marches

During the early '30s I was regularly unemployed for short periods as were many others of my generation. It was also the time of the stringent means test so that if a man was unemployed and claiming for his wife and family he could expect a home visit from the authorities who would carefully inspect his furniture and property. If there was a piano then they were told it had to be sold before they could be given benefit. Any property or possessions a family had managed to build up during a lifetime of work were taken away from them, and people were very bitter about it. You had to be a real pauper to draw benefit as well as suffer the indignities of the means test. It was not merely a question that you were not able to have the luxuries of life but you were not even able to get the essentials. People were hungry, distressed and full of despair and it is surely a dreadful period in our history as a nation that we failed to provide even the barest of necessities for the people who suffered unemployment.

In the summer months large numbers of single young men in the Chesterfield area used to leave home, get a tent and live rough so they could claim they were living away from home and qualify for their own benefit. Otherwise if the means test calculated there was sufficient income for the family and you were living at home you would not get any benefit even though you were out of work. It was also necessary to physically attend to sign on. If you weren't there then they said you were not available for work and therefore got no money. Mind you, we were fighting with thousands just to get signed on because there were so many unemployed. At Grassmoor because there were so many miners either on short-time or out of work they used to have to hire the club room at the back of the pub so people could sign on. It was the only way they could deal with the numbers involved.

It was in this atmosphere that the National Unemployed Workers Movement developed and began to have a real effect. In essence it was the only organisation campaigning against the Tories and their attacks on the unemployed. And because everyone had to go to the labour exchange twice a week to sign on, the NUWM used to use it as a chance to make contact with everyone. We used to get a box and have propaganda meetings and were able to set up advice centres and take individual cases to the means test tribunal, often managing to get benefits re-instated.

The NUWM also organised the mass demonstrations in protest at the labour exchange's working card rule. Because the exchanges demanded evidence that you were genuinely seeking work they used to issue you with a green card and every time you saw an employer for a job, he used to have to sign it to verify you had been. Then, when the exchange asked where you had been to look for work, you had to present your card or they could stop your benefit. So the NUWM mobilised the unemployed, all with their green cards, into mass demonstrations and swooped on factories and the like who then had to sign up to 500 green cards a time for the crowd gathered outside their gates. Which is why the system was eventually scrubbed because the employers complained they could not afford to employ clerks just to sign the labour exchanges' cards.

Each member of the NUWM had a stamped membership card and paid a penny a week and I devoted most of my time and energies to be with the unemployed. I took part in speaking at the labour exchanges and organised numerous meetings with the trade union and labour organisations to try to win their support as the NUWM was the only organisation trying to organise the unemployed into an effective opposition force against the government. But we were never able to get either the local Constituency Party or the local Trades Council to participate effectively and officially in organising the marches. Even when some of the national hunger marches were passing through to London I can't recall of any occasion when the local labour movement ever participated in arrangements either to receive or feed the marchers.

The NUWM had branch secretaries and various rooms from which we operated, which were loaned to us by all sorts of people. I remember one being on Low Pavement and another in Falcon's Yard in Chesterfield, while another was an old mission on Derby Road. But mainly we were at the labour exchanges meeting people and sorting out their problems. Nationally, the NUWM organised publicity-seeking stunts and demonstrations to draw the public's attention to the unemployed's situation, such as when a number of them went to the Savoy and other luxury hotels and lay down in their foyers, and on demonstrations we carried a black coffin with the words on the side:"He died on the UAB", referring to the Unemployed Assistance Board.

Of course the most notorious events were the hunger marches where men marched to various places on a district, regional and national basis. It is a myth to believe that Jarrow was the only, the first or the best hunger march. The Jarrow march was at the end of the period and there had been many national hunger marches before it, and countless hunger marches in which the unemployed had demonstrated against their conditions. But Jarrow was significant in that it had the support of the town council and its MP Ellen Wilkinson, whereas on a lot of the other occasions when we organised national hunger marches our weakness showed in that the NUWM did not get the fundamental backing from the main stream and main organisations of the labour movement. The TUC turned its back on the unemployed and would not have any organisational or effective co-operation with the unemployed and refused to back either the NUWM marches or to organise marches themselves.

So we used to try to raise sufficient money so that if someone's shoes were deteriorating to the point where they could not march any more, we could probably provide them with a new pair. Unlike today, most of those marching had never been out of their home town in their lives and had certainly never been away from home for any period of time. So the fact that they were prepared to go and join the march at say, Sheffield or Chesterfield and go to London without proper clothing, leaving their families for two or three weeks to demonstrate their hostility towards the government and demand a better and fairer deal, shows the depth of feeling there must have been. You had to have the courage of your convictions and everything else to participate in those marches. Because the labour movement was not as well organised then as it is today the marchers faced very rough feeding and sleeping arrangements. Bread and cheese or jam were the main staple diet and often the local workhouse the only place to sleep, although this was not always accomplished with ease.

I remember Dai Lee, secretary of the Nottinghamshire and Derbyshire district of the NUWM, a little man who generally wore no teeth and looked nearly emaciated but who had a powerful voice and who was a wonderful organiser and great orator. He was in charge of marchers in this area who, on this particular occasion, were about to arrive in Cheltenham. Someone had been sent on in front to see if they could contact anyone or any organisation prepared to accommodate or make arrangements for the marchers. No one was, including the workhouse master who felt the sooner we got out of his town the better. So Dai sent someone down to the local library to do some research into where the workhouse master lived.

Unemployed workers Marching for Jobs in 1981 as their fathers and grandfathers had done in the 1930's.

35

Armed with this information Dai then diverted the 200 marchers to a western suburb of the town, found the workhouse master's home and announced that he either found them all a place in the workhouse or they would camp out in his front garden. It didn't take him long to agree to make the necessary arrangements at the workhouse!

In Chesterfield I recall once having to enlist the help of the police. We had been unable to make arrangements for the impending marchers and advised the police to come up with a solution or have 200 tired and hungry men on their hands. They put us on to one of the religious organisations — I believe it was the Assembly of God — where Pastor Smith had a hall somewhere at the back of Low Pavement. And they happily fed the men and allowed them to sleep there in return for a religious service in the evening. But seeing as they picked some hymns we could all sing it only added to the entertainment rather than distract from it. They were marvellous people and it has to be said that this was one occasion where the church and the police provided us with more help than the local Labour party.

CHAPTER TWELVE

Fascists

Oswald Mosley recognised that the attitude of the 1930 Labour government was not going to present any results that would affect the people or regenerate industry to provide reasonable conditions for the unemployed. So he resigned from the Labour cabinet and developed a campaign which ultimately led to the formation of what he called the New Party. By 1933 this had developed into a semi-military fascist movement with supporters dressed in black shirts with all the apings of Mussolini. Although it cannot be said that the normal labour movement played a leading part in it they preferred, as usual, not to start any campaign against it in the belief it would only create disturbances and argued that it was better to leave the fascists alone. This meant, of course, that they got a free field so it was primarily the Left in the movement who developed the anti-fascist campains.

One of those most attracted by Mosley's programme for the unemployed was Vin Williams who joined the New Party in its early days. And I remember sitting listening enthralled to Vin's accounts of the occasions he went to London to attend meetings of Mosley's Council or confederates. Vin was looked upon as a real catch because he was one of the few ordinary and genuine working class people involved in the New Party. Most of the others were so called intellectuals and Mosley, being a wealthy man, used to organise dinner parties and invite Vin, who would tell you stories of how he would try to cope with being there. In 1931 the New Party decided to put up election candidates, and Vin was selected to stand in the North East Derbyshire constituency. Obviously he did not get many votes and lost his deposit. Once Vin realised Mosley was going down the trail to the formation of a fascist party he left and denounced the New Party for all it was worth. But the damage for him personally had already been done and it took him many, many years to overcome this episode of his life.

It is to be remembered, of course, that one of the things which Hitler used as a so called propaganda instrument was the supposed solving of the unemployment problem by putting people back to work. And this is still a dangerous argument today. So it was necessary for the labour movement in Britain to develop an anti-fascist movement. I believe one of the tragedies in the early years of the International labour movement was the destruction of the German working class, in the sense that it was achieved by the right wing reactionary forces because of the disunity and refusal to accept the danger of fascism. As a result they were able not only to destroy the Communist party but the Social Democratic Party and, ultimately, the liberal parties and the trade union movement. Everything in opposition to capitalism and reaction was destroyed on the basis of this so called popular movement.

In the East Midlands Mosley organised some big meetings in Nottingham,whose industry was based on textiles and where there was a concentration of Jews. We in the Left, particularly those of us in the

National Unemployed Workers Movement, organised campaigns for rallies against Mosley especially when we learned of his plans to hold a mass demonstration and meeting inside the town's Albert Hall, the largest hall in Nottingham. The only way we had of letting people know about our rally was to rely on our system of chalking. This involved obtaining some big lumps of chalk which were used to write on street corners the time and venue of our meeting. It effectively mobilised the people and, unlike the modern fly-postering, did not disfigure the place for long after the event. It was illegal, of course, so we had to do it when the police were not watching. But while Jock Kane and I were chalking on one of the Nottingham pavements advertising our rally against the fascists, the police came and arrested us and charged us with defacing the road and pavement. So we were taken to the station and eventually sent summonses to appear in court at a given date after the rally was held.

But we went to the rally and spoke outside, then went into the Albert Hall meeting, which was in the main hall which had swing doors then a number of steps. It was arranged that we would question a number of statements that were being made but unfortunately, with hindsight, I picked a seat that was the least favourable for me to be in. Before we got to the stage where questions were raised or we could make an interjection these tough, rough guys who had been specially recruited and paid to throw out any interjectors, grabbed us from the back and pulled us over the top of our seats. Eventually I found myself on the pavement at the bottom of the flight of steps, and they hadn't bothered to open the doors when they threw me — you opened the doors as you were being thrown through them. It took me about a week to get over the bruises.

In Chesterfield we had not seen much activity from the fascists but they suddenly announced they were going to organise a mass meeting in the market hall with Raven Thompson, Mosley's second in command, as the main speaker. We discussed what we should do and decided the best way that we could approach it was to organise an outdoor meeting on the pump outside the hall in the main market place, and start it about an hour before their meeting arguing against fascism. It was a good tactic so long as you had sufficient speakers to keep the thing going. In our case there was only Jock and myself and in those days we had no loud speakers, so it was a terrific job to try to keep a crowd and speak above the traffic and other noises.

We started out at about half-past-six and kept going on and on and on until about nine o'clock when we thought we had managed to succeed in preventing people from going inside to the other meeting. But apparently the fascist brigade, and I think most of them had been brought in from outside, were standing waiting in the market hall for us to finish and as soon as we indicated that we had, they rushed onto the pump to harangue the crowd who we had kept there all that time. So we then had to mobilise the crowd to throw them off the pump, which we managed to do but it meant that we had to re-start our meeting and start speaking again. We managed it until about ten o'clock when the police arrived and it was one of the few occasions when

I felt grateful to see them. I remember an old sergeant coming over to me and telling me that if I didn't get something done about my throat it would be ruined for life. It was sore and hoarse and although he made it clear he did not agree with what we were doing he insisted on sending me down to the hospital to have it sprayed.

It may be due to pure old age, but I believe I still suffer some effect from that incident because if I talk for a long time or go to a function where I have to raise my voice I normally find when I get home my voice is affected.

CHAPTER THIRTEEN

1933 Clay Cross By-election

In 1933 Charlie Duncan the Labour MP for the Clay Cross division died and created what eventually became known as a famous by-election. As his death came shortly after the '31 election, in which a large number of MPs lost their seat, the party's national headquarters decided they wanted to put up General Secretary Arthur Henderson for the seat. Henderson was referred to by the press and others as Uncle Arthur, but I'm afraid that amongst the normal workers — particularly the left wing of the movement — there were no such affectionate terms used when they described him.

Previously there had been arguments within the movement about the necessity of maintaining miner MPs or miners' representation, and the miners looked upon Clay Cross as one of the places where they thought their influence and standing demanded it be a miners' nominee who stood in the town. The party's national headquarters, however, decided that the safe Labour seat was to be used to put Henderson back into parliament and accordingly instructed the local Labour people who were arranging the election conference to accept him as one of the nominees. Apparently the national headquarters then sent up people who not only resurrected local parties and provided them with delegates credentials, but actually arranged the birth of a few so they could have the required number of delegates at the selection conference. So in the end, even though Sam Sales the Derbyshire Miners Association Vice-president had been the Labour party nominee, Arthur Henderson became the official candidate.

In view of the political situation and the fact that Clay Cross was a solid Labour seat, the Communist party declared it would put up its own candidate and nominated its General Secretary Harry Pollitt, while the Tories selected John Moores, one of the Littlewoods Pools family, as their candidate. As Henderson was General Secretary of the Labour party the campaign obviously drew national attention with people coming in from all parts of the country to campaign. Because I was one of the few people who knew about the Clay Cross constituency I was elevated, either fortunately or otherwise, to a leading role in the operation and clearly remember being given the job of going to see Sam Sales to discuss the situation with him.

Accompanying me to Tupton was Arthur Horner who was unemployed and actively involved in left-wing politics. We were both given our bus fares and because Sam knew Arthur well through his activities with the mineworkers he lavished hospitality on to Arthur, providing him with a bottle or two of beer. But although I was 23, Sam judged I was too young to be allowed a heavy sip of the brown liquid so I had to be given lemonade. We discussed the election and it was from Sam that we elicited the information of the gerrymandering that had taken place to provide Arthur Henderson with his seat. Sam declared that if he had any influence then never again would he allow an outsider to be brought into the election field. When it came to time to leave I had to remind Arthur that it was a considerable distance back to Clay Cross and although he might have been very pleased with the fact he had been given a bottle or two of brown ale, we had no bus fare to get home and perhaps he ought to use his further influences with Sam to provide us with the bus fare!

Another one of my jobs was to act as a 'minder' to John Strachey, who eventually became an MP in the Labour cabinet and played a leading role within the Attlee government. But at that time he was on the left wing of the movement and came up to Clay Cross to give his full support to Pollitt in the election. I remember him asking me to provide him with some accommodation somewhere in the country as he wanted to enjoy the Derbyshire countryside. Eventually I came across the Greyhound pub at Milltown near Ashover and Strachey was extremely pleased to stay there as one of the Penguin paperback mystery stories called Murder at the Greyhound had been written around the pub and its location.

John Strachey also wrote books and is remembered for a magnificent little pamphlet he wrote for the Left Book Club about Why You Should Be a Socialist. It was a wonderful statement of what socialism is all about and sold around a million copies at twopence each. And it is my view that if the Labour party resurrected it and sold it for fivepence a copy and made an effort to sell it, it would have a tremendous effect on the movement. Strachey eventually wrote a later book called the Coming Struggle for Power, which is a first class book on the understanding of why it is that a Social Democratic government or Labour government always fails when they come to the crunch of having to attack and destroy capitalism, when their very composition and philosophy crumbles to pieces. Anyway, he was very grateful to me for finding him this wonderful accommodation and as way of thanks invited me to visit him and his family down south, but I never attempted to take him up on it.

Because the campaign was during a period of good weather we had many open air meetings during which Pollitt spoke to hundreds of people. And I recall an incident which in later years Pollitt always used to rib me about. It was decided to hold an open air meeting on Shirland Green and my task was to go and get a box and put it up, announce and start the meeting in preparation for Pollitt to speak to the people. So I got my box, put it up and started to speak. Eventually people opened their doors and came and stood or sat on their steps. And I hollered and bellowed for about an hour trying to collect this crowd. Then Pollitt turned up, got on the box and, of course, everybody became interested so he asked them to come a bit closer and they came across. At the end of the meeting he took me to one side and said, "That's how you have to do it, lad. There's no need for all this shouting". At which point he claims I lost my temper and told him that if he had been there a bloody hour before hand he wouldn't have had a crowd.

In Clay Cross at that time there was what they called the Long Rows, which were long rows of cottages with toilets across the yard — actually, they were middens — where people were solidly staunch Labour in principle which they thought was being loyal to their class. So they became confused in relation to the problems that were posed when a Communist candidate entered the field in what they believed was opposition to the Labour party and the labour movement. They were very hostile at the beginning of the campaign and we couldn't get a meeting organised in the Long Rows and were even chased out of it a couple of times. The women there would make, and dye brilliantly red, enormous pairs of women's knickers on which they then printed something like 'We Want Henderson In' to hang on clothes lines between the middens on one side and the houses on the other. So there would be quite a lot of them down this long row.

But in truth Henderson had no more in common with the people in the Long Rows than the Tory candidate. He was equally far away and would be equally useless to them in their representation. But they didn't understand that and believed what they were doing was in the general interest of the working people. One day Pollitt came up to me in the committee rooms and said: "Come tomorrow we are going down the Long Rows". I said, "Who is?" and he said: "We are. You know this area and you are going with me down the Long Rows". Despite my protestations he insisted I went with him and a team of ordinary people. And we went. We explained to the women that all we wanted to do was meet them. Pollitt got a lot of banter from them and I remember there were a lot of children running about, with the women asking Pollitt: "What can you do about these?" pointing to the youngsters. Eventually they provided us with an old kitchen chair and Pollitt got up and said the best method of birth control that he and his wife Marjorie had discovered was when he was sent down the line to prison. It broke the ice and they listened and applauded and we never had any more trouble throughout the campaign about going down the Long Rows.

This was typical of Pollitt. While he was a brilliant politician and wonderful orator he also had the common touch. He could go anywhere workers were and meet them on their own terms and produce a response from them. He was born and brought up in Manchester and regarded by people who heard him or lived in his times as the best political orator that we ever had.He could do it either on a street corner meeting or in the biggest halls in the country. He was my great hero and I cherished the fact that he regarded me as a sort of friend and special person with whom he could communicate. Pollitt was an individual who was not only a great dedicated politician but also a great human being. Above everything else he was always concerned about the people in the movement, particularly the old.

He argued strongly about the movement being soulless in the sense it accepted everything certain people could give when they were active in life and participating in the movement with all their strength, but as soon as they were old or no longer able to participate then no one ever seemed to bother about them. He argued that this should not happen and that everybody, whatever sphere they were in in the movement, should take time to go and see the old or sick. And he practiced what he preached. For I recall an old propagandist called Bill Gee who used to go around meetings getting a shilling or two here and there. Eventually he fell on hard times, became old without money and starving. So Pollitt wrote to some of the leading people in the movement who had known Bill and asked for contributions on a regular basis. He collected this money then regularly went to see Bill to give him it as a small pension, and to make sure he had sufficient to eat and a place to live.

It is an example of the kind of person Pollitt was. With his ability and capabilities he could have had any job in the Labour movement that he wanted. But he spurned all the so called ambitious jobs of getting on in the movement so he could maintain his principles. As far as I was concerned Pollitt was the Lord God and if I could match any of his qualities and principles I should be content because he was one of the few working class politicians who honoured all the principles he set out to proclaim. It's my prejudiced view that the movement, particularly the Communist Party, has never been the same since he died for there has never been the same sort of inspired leadership that he gave.

Arthur Henderson had been Foreign Secretary and was the leading light of the labour movement, who brought their national agents into Clay Cross to fight a vicious campaign against the Communists based on the red bogey men. He was propped up and carried about like a corpse and was certainly half-dead during the course of the by-election, which he eventually won. But the local party people were incensed by the national organisation and declared they would never again have a candidate foisted upon them. So a group of Labour people and the Left got together to pick their own local candidate who they would support at the next election. And I was approached to join the Labour party and become their nominee for the next election. Obviously I wasn't prepared to besmirch my purity and change over, but I did join in their discussions and was partly responsible for suggesting that they should approach a comrade in Tibshelf called Alf Holland, who was branch manager of the local Co-op and who was sunbsequently adopted as the next Labour party candidate and became the area's MP after Henderson's death. Unfortunately he was only in the House of Commons for about two years when he had a brain tumour and died even though he was quite a young man. Then the pendulum turned again because the right wing took its revenge and palmed off an outsider on the party called George Ridley who was a railway clerk — and you can never get anyone more right wing than a railway clerk!

It was only after this that the NUM was able to come in and claim Clay Cross a mining seat. And since that time, in spite of the changes in constituency boundaries, it has traditionally remained a mining seat. The Clay Cross constituency, which took in Tibshelf and South Normanton, became part of the Bolsover constituency, although Clay Cross itself went into North East Derbyshire which enabled the miners to establish the two constituencies as mining seats. This tradition was ultimately maintained by Harold Neale in Clay Cross and Harry White in North East Derbyshire, with Tom Swain and Ray Ellis following White and Dennis Skinner following Neale.

However in the course of writing this book it is interesting to note that Harry Barne's election in 1987 broke the tradition in North East Derbyshire.

CHAPTER FOURTEEN

The Kane Family

The Kanes were one of the most amazing and unique families that I ever had the experience to meet because not only were the whole of the family dedicated to the working class movement, but all of them devoted a terrific amount of time, ability and sincerity to it. This was a family which originated in Fife in Scotland and because of their activities in the pits around Fife they were victimised and blacked throughout the whole of the Scottish coalfield. So they walked from Fife into Durham to try to get a job in the coalfield there, but were unsuccessful. Eventually they moved down into Yorkshire and Derbyshire, arriving in Staveley on the outskirts of Chesterfield around 1929. They were a large close-knit family and it was said that they hunted and worked in packs. There was Martin, John (Jock), Mick, Mary, Bridget, Patrick and various children and in-laws connected with them, so they normally needed two or three houses to fit them all in.

Martin Kane was the eldest in the family and looked upon as the patriarch. He was a man sick with tuberculosis and never worked because of his condition but was nevertheless considered the head of the family. He was the theoretical director of the various campaigns who acted as adviser until his death in 1948. Jock, Mick and Patrick got jobs in Staveley pits and started organising and recruiting to establish trade union membership, which had become slack after the 1926 strike. They were agitating for improved wages and conditions within the pits around this time and were joined by a number of others, including Tom Swain who later became MP for North East Derbyshire. To help their campaign they started publishing what was known as the Staveley Sparks, which was a small duplicated sheet which sold for a half-penny and which used to highlight the problems and difficulties of the miners at the pit.

After a time the company, for one reason or excuse, gave them all the sack. The Kanes were all living in Staveley Company houses in the square at Poolsbrook when the company decided to make an example of them and sent out eviction notices to the Kanes and about a dozen other families in Poolsbrook. Some were for arrears of rent but so far as the Kane family was concerned it was because it was a company house and let on the basis that they were employees of the company, which they were now no longer. So they were told to get out and although a number of other families were also given eviction notices, the company's prime concern was to evict the Kanes who they wanted to be rid of.

When the bailiffs came to turn them and their furniture out of the house Martin was sick in bed, so they carried him out in his bed. The only place he could be taken to was hospital but the authorities said that they were homeless and therefore the responsibility of the Lothian authorities in Scotland and that they ought to go back there. So they turned to the relieving officer who, under the old poor law system, had the authority to admit

Chesterfield Workhouse which operated until the mid 1940s when the NHS came along and turned it into Scarsdale Hospital, a geriatric and, until 1989, maternity hospital.

people into the workhouse or provide relief of one sort or another, and pleaded with him to find them some shelter. Mick, Jock and the sons of the family argued for Martin to go to the hospital but finally agreed to sign the admitting document to the workhouse, which was at Scarsdale Hospital. Mick, Jock and the rest of the men had to make their own living arrangements, and the Staveley Company issued a warning to all the other residents in their company properties that if any of them took in the evicted families they would be similarly dealt with as they would be in breach of contract. But there was a Salvation Army family who thought this was against all their principles of Christian brotherhood and they did provide lodgings for some of the men.

The women and children were taken into the workhouse but because of the rules and regulations young children in given ages were not allowed, so most were sent to the children's home at Brampton. As soon as they got to the workhouse Mary, Bridget and Annie, who had experience of battling in the working class movement, asked for a book of rules and proceeded to exploit it for all they were worth. For example they found out that the authorities had to provide access for them to see the children and so about once a week a taxi would bring them to the workhouse. And young Bridget, who was about eleven at the time, says that while it must have been a traumatic experience it was full of excitement and at least they got three good meals a day which they never did outside. Each weekend the staff would get them ready to see their parents and they got this ride in a taxi, which was beyond their wildest dreams in normal life.

They were in these conditions for eight weeks, partly because the authorities were arguing over whose responsibility the family were and trying to send them back to the Lothian area and Fife in Scotland. Bridget believes they had their travel vouchers ready when some landlord in Staveley was persuaded to let them have a big house on Chesterfield Road which had three floors, and all three families went and lived and shared it. The astonishing thing is what all these people eventually turned out to be.

Mick Kane could not get back into the pits so he went to lodge with a Scottish family in Harworth and eventually got a job at the local colliery. There he and others set up a branch of the Nottinghamshire Miners Association in opposition to the Spencer union. The company said it would negotiate only with the Spencer union but Mick led the battle for the re-establishment of normal trade union activities. Eventually they built up a campaign in support of these proposals and in 1937 they forced a ballot amongst the Harworth miners on which trade union they wanted to be a member of, and there was overwhelming majority amongst the miners to form the Nottingham Miners Association rather than Spencerism. The company refused to accept this, which led to what has become known in working class history as the Harworth dispute when the miners at Harworth came out on strike and a terrific battle took place between the men who wanted to form the Nottinghamshire Miners Association and the company and the few scabs who continued working supporting Spencerism.

The issue was fought out in the mining village with a tremendous spirit among the miners and strikers. A large police presence became common as the black-legs were escorted down the pit lane between solid ranks of policemen on either side. The women of the village used to go down to the lane and "pan them in", which involved carrying dustbin lids, saucepans and the such which they then proceeded to rattle and bang to create a terrific din as the scabs walked through the ranks. As in other disputes, the police used to try to provoke the miners and as a result Mick went to prison for three years. He was the mildest mannered individual it was your fortune to meet but obviously he was an inspiring leader and when he appeared to try and quell some disturbance which was taking place he was arrested and charged as the leader of the affray and ultimately got his jail sentence.

But the fact is that arising out of the Harworth dispute there developed a campaign throughout the whole of the labour movement, particularly among the miners, for a national strike in support of the Harworth people to re-establish the authority and right of the old Nottinghamshire Miners Federation. Because of this there were national negotiations and ultimately an agreement between the Federation of Miners nationally on the joining together of certain terms of the Spencer union and the Nottinghamshire miners, which then became part of the Miners Federation. So by and large it was due to the battle that Mick Kane and his colleagues fought at Harworth that formed the basis on which the national unity of the Miners Federation of Great Britain was re-established. When Mick came out of prison he obviously was not allowed back his old job, so he came back in to Derbyshire, got a job at Grassmoor colliery and eventually became a full time official of the Derbyshire Miners Association.

After the eviction Jock Kane played an important part in the local Chesterfield movement, especially in the National Unemployed Workers Movement and the anti-facist struggle. He went to the Lenin School in the Soviet Union for two years and on his return became a full-time organiser for the Communist party in Sheffield. But all the time he really wanted to return to his first love which was mining, and eventually went in to the Yorkshire coalfield and got a job at Armthorpe. Because of his abilities he quickly became one of the leading miners and a local agent which looked after a number of pits. When the government took over the mining industry prior to nationalisation because of the war situation it set up various organisations in the coalfield similar to the present Area Management Committees. Jock was appointed as one of the labour officers for one of the regions in Yorkshire, who we would today call a personnel manager. But it was completely foreign to what he believed his role in life should be, so he eventually resigned because he said he could not stand to be part of the management set up. His whole sympathy and wishes were on the side of the men and all he wanted to do was get back into the pit and on to the coal face. They thought he was mad but I met him just after he had made this decision and he was so relieved to be going back in to the pit you would have thought he had won the pools. Eventually he became a leading figure in the Armthorpe mining circles and a full-time compensation agent for the Yorkshire miners and played a leading role within the NUM, especially after nationalisation.

The women of the family were also a tower of strength. Mary MacMahon played a full role in the labour movement and remained a member of the Labour party. She was a leading councillor during the days of the old Urban District Council at Staveley. Kate was good looking and had all her wits about her and went off to London where she went into service and eventually married an Italian with whom she set up a transport cafe. They willingly offered hospitality no matter how difficult the circumstances were and it was always an experience to go and stay there. She had a son, Adam, who was brought up by Bridget, affectionately known by all as "Aunty" Bridget.

Aunty Bridget never married but while Martin had been the patriarch, Bridget was the matriarch. She was the centre around which everything else spun. She brought up nephews and nieces and loved to run the home, and people looked to her with enormous respect. She was the guiding hand at the back of everybody and kept some place for them all to come back to if it were necessary. I remember being at Aunty Bridget's on one occasion for tea and she had some fancy pastries and when Jock went to get one of these cakes at the beginning, she reprimanded him and told him it was very bad manners and he shouldn't do that sort of thing, to which he replied that it might be bad manners but it was bloody good tactics because if you relied on practising your good manners you might be left out.

I first met the Kane family by being involved in the National Unemployed Workers Movement in the early '30s and eventually became very friendly with them and have since been connected with them all my life. They were a great family to be with and, at the time of writing, Aunty Bridget remains as bright as a button still living in Walton Road, Chesterfield where the family clan occasionally gathers from the four corners of the earth to where they have now spread.

CHAPTER FIFTEEN

1935-37 Lenin School

In the midst of my involvement with the National Unemployed Workers Movement I was sent for by the Communist party office in Sheffield to meet the then district organiser, whose name was Bill Joss. He suggested that in view of my activities and the necessity for a better understanding of the theory of the movement that I should go to the Soviet Union to what we knew as the Lenin School. This was a school which existed for teaching the theories and practices of the movement, particularly Marxism.

You can imagine what a traumatic decision it was to make because I had never been away from home very much in my twenty-five years and the family had no knowledge of people going away. To talk about leaving for two years, and particularly at this time to talk about going to the Soviet Union, was completely beyond all known human experience. But eventually I decided I would go and went, luckily, with the blessing of the family although they did not like it very much.

I remember I had to go to London to make a number of arrangements with people. A berth had been booked for me on a ship leaving from the London docks to Leningrad and while I was in London I met Harry Hicken walking along the street with Jim Griffiths, who was then one of the South Wales miners' leaders as well as an MP. He asked me where I was going and what I was doing in London and I explained that I was making arrangements to go to the Soviet Union. We were near London bridge and looking at the House of Commons and I recall commenting that the place had always intrigued me and that I would have liked to have been there. To which Harry Hicken said that if I had any real ambitions for being in the House of Commons then I was going about it the wrong way as it certainly would not be achieved by going to the Soviet Union, a view which Jim Griffiths thoroughly endorsed.

The first few days of being aboard that ship were some of the most miserable days that I have ever had in my life. I was obviously nervous about travelling and arrived to claim my berth full of all the misgivings it was possible to have. And due to sea sickness I was hardly able to get out of the bunk. In those days I think it took five days to get to Leningrad, and it was probably about three days before I could come out of the cabin. I was just beginning to find my way about the ship when we got to Leningrad. After passing through customs I sat down and was approached by a little jovial fellow who spoke English, although not very well, who said he had been sent as my uncle and would take me to a hotel for a meal before putting me on a train to Moscow.

I've been to the Soviet Union on a number of occasions since this time and obviously enjoyed it very much. But on this first trip when I was completely on my own and not sure of what I would find or where I was going to be sent, it was a very unnerving situation. But I eventually got to Moscow and went to the Lenin School, which was set up for people from the various movements throughout the world. They included Americans, Britons, Australians, Germans, French, the colonial countries — in fact, most of the international world. Our main task was to study the development and history of our own particular movement but for me the biggest benefit I got from the experience was the chance to meet all these international comrades.

Some of the people I got along with best and really enjoyed were the Chinese comrades who were able to tell you the real practical problems they had because a number of them spoke very good English. One I was particularly friendly with looked as though his ears were chopped off from the side of his face and I remember asking him why this was so. He explained it was because he had been captured by the Kuomintang and they had hung him up by his ears and he had lost them. So when you were talking to people like this who were describing the development of their movement you were not talking to people who were in it for the kudos or because they believed this was a fanciful way of spending their spare time, but to people involved in true reality.

Similarly my understanding of the American movement was enchanced tremendously by the fact that I was able to meet and discuss with those Americans who were part and parcel of their movement and who could give me a full insight into their difficulties. Up until then I never realised the physical brutality which was practiced by the Pinkerton strike breakers on those trying to build up a labour movement in America. Much of the progressive and social literature of the '20s and '30s sprang from American writers and we must remember that May Day was originally launched in America by the IWW people, the Wobblies as they were called in the movement. One of the weaknesses today of the whole American system is that there is no real American labour movement that can express the desires of the ordinary working class folk and they are bogged down in the tweedle-dum tweedle-dee situation of the so called Republican and Democratic organisations, which do not express any aspirations of the ordinary people only the aspirations of different sets of the capitalist system. And I do not believe there will be a tremendous advance in the American situation unless they can develop some basic trade union movement.

In a way being at the Lenin school was a rather artificial experience in the sense that only on certain occasions were we part and parcel of Soviet society, while similarly being isolated from the movement back home. In the summer recess we were able to travel about the country as a Soviet delegation and got to see and do various things. I remember one May Day we went to a factory and joined their delegation on its march through Red Square, eating picnics and sandwiches on the road while we waited for our turn to go through the Square, which was all quite an experience. On another occasion I was seconded to the International Department where part of my job was to be allocated to various delegations visiting the Soviet Union so I could attempt to answer their questions and so they could at least meet someone from Britain. Many were from the British trade union movement and I noticed that the more reactionary they were in Britain, the more revolutionary they were when they got to the Soviet Union. It was mainly, of course, after a fair dose of good cognac. Nevertheless, some were real bloodthirsty characters who were ready to cleave their way across Europe with a sword. But if you reminded them about it later, they did not want to know.

Whenever the leading people in the movement came to Moscow, as they regularly did, then it became a statutory duty that they spoke to our international group of students. In that way I was able to meet Dimitrov Togliatti, the leader of the Italian communist party, Maurice Thorez, leader of the French CP and, on one occasion, Chou-en Lai for the Chinese CP, which was all a great experience. We also had the opportunity of going to the Bolshoi theatre regularly and seeing ballet and concerts. In some senses it was like a new life on a higher cultural level. We also got all the newspapers from around the world, and one of the curious by-products of this was that we got to know all the comings and goings about the Duke of Windsor and Mrs. Simpson months before it became knowledge back home. The American press would publish something about them every day while there was never a word in the British papers until the thing was blown by the Bishop of Bradford. This proved to everyone the power the press has on whether to publicise or censor a matter.

All the students had interpreters who could translate the Russian language into most other languages in common use throughout the world. Lessons were divided into nationalities and there was a big communal refectory where you served yourself and which provided all sorts of dishes. But once a month you had a room to yourself with the national dish. When it was the English national dish we had steak and chips and ice-cream and when the Americans had their national day they had steak and chips, so you would become American for the day. When the French had their national day they too had steak and chips, so then we would become French for the day, and so on. So it is a comment on the international eating habits that nearly everyone who wanted a national dish wanted steak and chips.

The international mix at the school included a group of Irish lads and because I expressed some interest in the Irish situation I was given the job of sort of convenor for the group and sat in with them discussing the pros and cons of the Irish situation. The whole Irish revolutionary movement is a complicated but interesting subject and these discussions gave me a great insight into the Irish problems and difficulties, as well as conclusively proving to me that there has been more revolutionary activity there than I think in any other movement in the world. Unfortunately it has not advanced the Irish working class one inch. The development of real working class organisations is completely lacking in Ireland and once again it has been left to either imperialist or religious feuds which, rather than advancing the Irish people's aspirations, have merely held them back. But I certainly got an understanding of what the situation there was, which I don't suppose I would have got unless I had been involved in this sort of activity.

During my two years in Moscow Harry Pollitt used to make regular trips to the city and I used to arrange to visit him at his hotel. It was on one of these early occasions that I remember him asking me if I was all right. I said yes, but that the letters I got from my mother seemed to indicate that she was worried about me. So I asked him if he would write to her telling her he had seen me and that I was okay as she probably thought I would never come back again. But when I got home I found out that he didn't write to my mother but that when he came up north for a meeting he told them to deliberately take him around to where I lived so he could go and see her personally. That was the sort of person Harry Pollitt was. That was what made him a great man.

When I first arrived in the Soviet Union there was bread rationing and I sometimes think people forget the tremendous struggle they had to rehabilitate a basically backward country which had nothing. I remember meeting some American comrades who were helping to build the Soviet metro who said that the lack of skilled labour was appalling. Those helping them build the metro were peasants who had never seen two bits of steel together in their life. Yet they had to try and train these people into engineers. So they had tremendous difficulties and it was the same with housing and everything else. The tragic thing was that they were just getting over this when it was all destroyed, with a whole generation of people aged between eighteen and thirty wiped out during the second world war. Around twenty million Soviets were killed, mostly the youngest and best who had just been trained, something no other country suffered. In one day the Soviets lost as many people as Britain lost during the whole of the war and few today understand the enormity of what that meant to everybody there. When anyone asks me about the Soviet Union's attitude towards peace and war I always say that if I were an ordinary Soviet citizen I would demand from my leaders that they say come what may, whatever the circumstances, whoever else has got to have a taste of it, then never again must the Soviet Union suffer as they did in the last war, never again must they be trampled over. And in my view that is the basis of their whole attitude formed on their experiences after the revolution and the last war.

CHAPTER SIXTEEN

Sheffield Organiser

When I got back from the Soviet Union in 1937 I was asked to report to the Communist party's North Midlands district office in Sheffield. At the time Jock Kane, who I have mentioned previously, was the party organiser in the city and when I turned up at the Bank Street office and opened the door and looked in, Jock was sitting at his desk. He turned around to see who had arrived and when he saw it was me said, "Thank God for that. Come on in", and got out of his chair and said, "Sit down there, that's yours". Apparently Jock was very anxious, for both personal and political reasons, to get back into the coalfields and there had been discussions in the party with the result that he was promised that as soon as I returned from the Soviet Union I would be his replacement. This I knew nothing about but it explains why Jock appeared to be so pleased to see me.

When I was told that my job was to be the Sheffield CP organiser I realised it would be a tremendous task for me. It was awe inspiring to discover that I, who had not had any previous job of this sort, was going to be pitchforked into a situation where I was virtually running the party in a city like Sheffield. Because, like most people, I was aware of the tremendous traditions and history of the Communist party, particularly in Sheffield which had a reputation and historical tradition in the British labour movement. It was Sheffield after the first world war that played a leading role in establishing a shop stewards movement in Britain, especially in the engineering industry. It also played an important role in the development of the struggles of the unemployment movement in the early '20s and, of course, was the first great city in Britain to have a Labour controlled majority in the municipal elections. Labour won Sheffield in 1926 and it has been Labour ever since, excepting for a brief aberration in 1970. So to be participating in this sort of situation was both a tremendous task and challenge to someone like myself who had not previously lived in the big city.

An organiser's job was similar to that of a secretary and so I organised meetings and did everything in an organisation that had to be done to run and maintain it. I would get people together to go out selling literature, distribute leaflets, issue circulars and organise meetings. You had to work at it constantly and there would be no let up from the moment you got in the office at about nine in the morning until ten or eleven o'clock at night. I got paid, but only as much as I was likely to have got on the dole, so had to rely absolutely on friends. The biggest difficulty was that the economic insecurity of the job meant you had to be constantly concerned about how you were going to live the next day, and under those kind of stresses and strains it was not always easy to concentrate on the real political nature of the job. I remember my staple diet for a long while was cheese and tomato sandwiches and eventually I broke out in boils and had to go home for a couple of weeks to get back on my feet before I could go to work again. The sacrifice was great. You just worked for as long as your health and strength held together because you hadn't got much else. Any hope of doing anything other than the job had to be put out of your mind as you could not afford it.

I remember on one occasion going with Jock to Harworth to discuss the strategy and tactics of the mining dispute there. When we got back we decided to scrape together what money we had got and see about getting something to eat. It amounted to something like one shilling and threepence, so we had tomatoes on toast and went back into the office. Waiting for us there was a colleague George Allison, and Jock sat on a chair and put his head in his hands. When George asked him what the matter was, Jock, who was very fond of classical music, replied he wished he had the fabulous fortune of half-a-crown so he could go and listen to the concert pianist Moiseiwich who was playing at the City Hall. George was so astonished and outraged he said, "Look mate, if we had a bloody half-a-crown we'd have a pint of bitter and listen to blind Harry on the fiddle". It was obviously idealistic to imagine that between the three of us we could raise half-a-crown (about twelve and a half pence today).

One of my saving graces over the problem of living was a family which ran a little lunch cafe on Cambridge Street which existed mainly by supplying meals to the people who worked for what was called the "little mesters", the people who did contract work for the cutlery industry. These were mainly small workshops with one, two or three people who did grinding or some of the small specialised jobs within the industry. There must have been literally hundred of these places in and around the alleys by Cambridge Street and Mrs. Furniss, who lived in one of these small two-up-two-down houses, turned her front room into a cafe where she supplied dinners for the people who worked in these various places.

She and her husband, who was naturally unemployed, were very interested in the labour movement and so used to make special concessions when it came to paying for the meal. The cafe's front room was where you sat and ate your mid-day meal and the other room was where they cooked it. Usually your main meal would cost ninepence and the sweet an extra threepence. But for those doing jobs for the movement, like party organisers, then we were given the full meal for just sixpence. It was cheap for someone paying the full price but for me it was a bonanza and I lived on it for the whole two years I was there. One of the things I liked about it best of all was that we agreed not to go in at their main mid-day period but later on when we would not be competing with the main customers. And if by chance the sweet had run out and it had been a steamed pudding or something then they would say, "Don't bother, we'll do you pancakes", and we would have pancakes and treacle which was a great boon. I used to end up hoping they would run out of sweet because you got this great plate of pancakes and treacle. Today the street has gone and where the cafe used to be lies part of the Cole Brothers store.

One of the campaigns organised during this time was a mass

unemployment demonstration to meet the then Minister of Labour who was going to speak to the assembled Tories in the City Hall. We arranged to have marches of people from the various districts in Sheffield who would then congregate in front of the City Hall, with meetings in the morning in all these areas as part of mobilising the demonstration. My job was to speak in Attercliff at the traditional meeting site by the corner of Attercliff Baths. We had called the meeting for about tenish in the morning and I got on my box and started to speak. At that particular moment a van, that we used to call a black Maria, arrived full of police who tumbled out and, before I knew where I was, I had been bundled off my box, thrown into the back of the van and taken away. I finished up, curiously enough, in an area in which I subsequently went to live which was Hillsborough, and was taken into the police station and put in a cell.

After a while the sergeant in charge of the station came down and took me to his office. Despite all my protestations and questions about why I had been held he issued a series of non commital replies that it was nothing to do with him, he wasn't involved and he didn't know why I was there except that obviously there had been some decision taken somewhere. There were a number of other people arrested and treated the same as I was on that day, presumably because the police believed that if they could behead the movement by lifting all the organisers this would affect the demonstration that was to take place outside the City Hall in the evening. It didn't because others stepped into our place and the massive demonstration in protest of how the Tory government treated the unemployed went ahead.

But one of the interesting things was that this old sergeant wanted to know if I knew anything about mining. I told him that in fact I had been employed in the industry for some short period of time and, to my astonishment, he went to a drawer and brought out all the newspaper cuttings and articles about the Gresford pit disaster in Wales and asked me if I could explain some of the diagrams. The incident had taken place earlier in the '30s and why he should have been interested in it was beyond comprehension because he didn't seem to have any connections with mining. But he had obviously become concerned in this particular tragedy in which more than a hundred people lost their lives. And he became very friendly towards me, even treating me as some sort of royalty in that he sent people out to get my meals from the local cafes. We spent the whole day discussing mines, mining area and the Gresford pit disaster until about nine at night when he suddenly said he had had instructions that I could be released, and that if he were me I should go home and be quiet and behave myself.

So I went to find out what had happened to everyone else and the demonstration. But it was unusual that here, to all intents and purposes, was a man with a social conscience who was concerned that people should have to earn their living in such a way as to expose to such dangers as were obvious in relation to the Gresford pit, and that all his sympathy was on their side. Luckily as an ex-miner this rubbed off on me a bit and I got some of his sympathy. He was probably the most human policeman that I have ever come across.

One of the great experiences of my stay in Sheffield was participating in the campaigning work. The Communist party took part in all the immediate issues of the day. It was the time when Hitler was beginning to dismember Europe and prepare for all out war; he moved into Czechoslovakia, Austria and attacked the People's government in Spain.

On each of these issues the party organised meetings and demonstrations, issued pamphlets and leaflets which were then distributed to the factories and around the housing estates. We also organised regular sales of the Daily Worker outside Woolworths on the Haymarket every Saturday, and when a new pamphlet came out we organised sales at the factory gates for the early morning shift, as well as on the early morning trams among the travelling workers. On Sunday mornings we would have a sales drive around the housing areas and when Hitler advanced into Austria, Harry Pollitt straight away wrote, and the party issued, a pamphlet calling on the government to take immediate steps to stop the Hitler advance to war. We sold a thousand copies within a week and held a tremendous protest meeting in Barker's Pool.

I believe the movement, both generally and nationally, misses great opportunities by not responding to the immediate issues more positively with pamphlets, leaflets, and meetings. While internal political discussions are important, it is the outgoing political activity and education that is going to be the key to success. This method of providing an immediate political response to the issue of the day heightened the political activity throughout the whole of the movement. You felt you were helping to shape the policy and future of the movement and were involving people in the decision. In this connection the weekly meetings at the political forum in Barker's Pool were most important.

Alongside Sheffield City Hall was an area where both political and religious organisations would raise their standards and speak to the people, very much like what occurs at Hyde Park Corner in London. It was a great training ground for would-be orators and politicians as on occasions there were as many as six meetings going on all at the same time, and you only got an audience if you were more interesting and a better speaker than the others. If you achieved success at Barker's Pool then I think you could rightly claim to be a public speaker.

I sometimes think it would not perhaps be a bad idea if some of our budding aspirants for councillors had to pass through a "Barker's Pool" training course. For nowadays, when public meetings seem to be out of fashion, there are some people able to climb to the dizzy heights of being a councillor without ever making a public speech in their life, let alone being able to use the platform of the Council to espouse and advance the cause of socialism.

Part of the job of being a party organiser was not only to see that the campaigns were run and that as many people as possible were activated and involved, but also to be ready to step into the breach and do any job that was called for. For me this meant a regular speaking commitment in Barker's Pool at the weekend because if we had not been able to book a speaker, or the one booked had not turned up, then the honour of being the standard bearer was mine. Curiously, all the talk these days of police surveillance, MI5 and "Spy catcher" reminds me of the fact that back in those days we never held a public meeting without two representatives of the CID being present. In fact in 1938 we discovered that some of their under cover men had even been attending our private meetings. I can only hope that their political education and development improved. The two who used to attend our public meetings were regularly on duty in Barker's Pool on Sundays and became regarded as fixtures. Indeed, if we saw them walking towards our meeting place we used to explain to the crowd that we could not start until Ward and Spencer were in position so they could take a full report back to their superiors.

It was about this time that the national newspaper wholesalers boycotted the Daily Worker newspaper and, for political reasons, refused to deliver it to the newsagents. This meant that the local party organisations had to set up their own distribution network. In Sheffield we got agreement with the newsagents to handle the paper and so it was our task to get the paper from the railway station to the newsagents' shops. We had a comrade, Les Baswell, who undertook this task which required him to be at the railway station between two and three o'clock in the morning. After collecting the papers he then set out on his bicycle to deliver the papers to the newsagents across Sheffield, and for this arduous task he was rewarded with the wholesaler's commission. Judged on the number of copes of the Daily Worker involved, I can assure you that this was not very much at all and only his devoted dedication allowed the paper to be distributed.

But whenever Les was taken ill or in anyway unable to carry out this duty he would ring the party office and tell me he would not be delivering the papers the next day. This left me with the problem of finding another distributor or doing the job myself. As you can imagine, it was more than difficult at short notice to find a replacement for Les, so I generally ended up by having to appear at the station myself at 2.30 in the morning. At least he was generous enough to lend me his bike, but it still burns in my memory the trauma of finding out just how hilly Sheffield is, delivering the papers and making sure I was in the office by 9 o'clock.

After a few of these experiences I managed to persuade a comrade who had a car to volunteer to accompany me on these excursions. This eased the problem tremendously and allowed us to get over the emergencies until the wholesaler problem was resolved with the outbreak of the war. In Chesterfield, though, we were never able to reach agreement with the newsagents so a local comrade, Bill Cairney, used to collect the papers from the town's railway station and then deliver them individually to the customers. Only in this way was the Daily Worker able to exist based solely on the enthusiasm and dedication of such people.

Looking back, being a party organiser was a fulfilling and a mentally and physically taxing job. But it was the one I was proud to do. The trust, confidence and respect that developed between other comrades was a tremendous experience and the lessons I learned from being involved in such an active political atmosphere have remained with me all my life.

In later life when I have seen comrades scrambling and battling for jobs, declaring that their only thought was how they could contribute and advance the movement without any thought of self-aggrandisement, I wonder how many would opt for the basic jobs in the movement — particularly as they were in the '30s. While I must confess I got great personal satisfaction from the jobs I did, realistically it was very hard even, on occasions, desperate. Your faith in the movement was indeed tested.

CHAPTER SEVENTEEN

George Fletcher

George Fletcher is recognised as probably one of the best known and best loved figures in the Sheffield labour movement for a generation or more. He had set out in life as a baker and when he became unemployed in the early 1900s and victimised he set up a little bakery of his own which eventually grew into a thriving business which still exists and is run by his grandson.

As a life-long Communist party member George always insisted that his people were employed under the best conditions, and in the early years when the bakers came out on national strike demanding better conditions he shut down his own bakery and put himself at the head of the demonstration and marched in support of the bakers' demands. It was actions like this, which were genuine and sincere, that endeared him to the people in the working class movement in Sheffield. He was a popular speaker and a good propagandist and used to claim that despite him being a leading Sheffield industrialist, the only time he went to the Cutlers Feast was the time he took 20,000 unemployed workers with him to demonstrate outside, and none was allowed to go in.

Sometimes I used to go to the bakery to discuss problems with him there and we would always have a cup of tea and fresh cake on the pretext that he wanted to try out some new cake which they had baked. While I was there on one of these occasions some police detectives came to see George and reported that they had caught some young lads aged about ten who had climbed over the wall and stolen some buns out of the bread vans. The police were keen for George to issue a summons against them, but he wanted to know who the boys were and where they lived. They were all from poor working class areas so George refused to take action against them. Instead, he told the police to get them together, give them a talking to and, if necessary, "kick their arse and send them on their way", adding: "We don't want to be talking about summonses for lads who are living in those sort of conditions and as far as I'm concerned that's the end of it". And despite desperate persuasion from the police for him to take action, George would not budge.

Among his various passions, George was a great Sheffield Wednesday supporter and although he did not mind attending meetings any day or evening of the week, Saturday afternoons were sacrosanct when, come what may, he would go to watch Sheffield Wednesday. And it became a common sight for a row of unemployed supporters to stand outside the ground waiting for George to appear when, generally speaking, he used to pay for the first six to go into the ground with him. He became one of the few Communist party members elected on to the Board of Guardians which issued relief to the unemployed, and used to fiercely argue their case for them.

I remember walking once with him up to the old Sheffield Independent offices where we had to pass the city's Cathedral which was in the process of being extended. As we passed it I mentioned to George that despite all the unemployment and poverty they could nevertheless afford to extend the Cathedral, to which he replied: "But at least I managed to delay the work for twenty years". Aware of George's well known agnostic principles, I couldn't understand what he had got to do with preventing work being done on the Cathedral. So he explained that when they first mooted the idea of extending the Cathedral the Lord Lieutenant of the County — who was then Lord Lascelles who married Princess Mary, the King's sister — called a special meeting in the city to launch the appeal. George presumes that somebody was given the task of sending out the invitations and had a list of business people taken from the business directory, and as head of Fletcher's Bakery George was invited to the meeting. Chairing it was Lord Lascelles who was about to propose launching the appeal for a certain target figure when George innocently asked if he would accept an amendment. Lord Lascelles, who presumably thought the amendment would probably increase the figure, agreed and was no doubt horrified to hear George propose that the appeal should not proceed until every worker had a decent house to live in and every parson had a decent stipend to live on. All the parsons at the meeting supported his amendment and so when it came to the vote the extension had to be abandoned for a considerable period of time!

He told me this story as we made our way to the Sheffield Independent to talk to reporters about the launch of the first national pamphlet published on what the authorities should be doing in face of a threat of outbreak of war. I suppose it must have been around the end of 1938 and the Sheffield party had collected a number of people together to discuss and produce what became the first of many Air Raid Precaution pamphlets which looked at what should be done in the city in relation to shelters and such, largely based on the work of Professor J.B.S. Haldane who also developed the idea nationally. During his discussions with the reporters George revealed he was going to America the following week to see his brother and relatives, and the next morning's headlines read: "Sheffield Communist to visit America". This was picked up by the American consul in Sheffield, reported to the Embassy who immediately withdrew George's visa. So we ran a terrific campaign to get the visa restored and got all the leading politicians and businessmen, such as the Lord Mayor, to sign a petition on his behalf. Eventually the authorities agreed but only after George signed an undertaking not to attend any political meetings or make any political speeches during his visit. George said he never had any such intentions and the only purpose of his visit was to see friends and relatives on holiday. But it highlights the fact that the mere mention of a Communist party member going to America could produce such a reaction from the American authorities who never initially questioned the purpose of his visit.

Whenever we had a big meeting at the City Hall or a march or demonstration, heading it would be an old Irish woman with a shawl around her head called Kate. What her second name was I never knew and I don't suppose anybody else knew it either. But George had a special arrangement with Kate so she could go into one of his retail shops and get a free loaf of bread whenever she needed one. And on Fridays she used to go to the bakery's office and draw half-a-crown which was typical of George who, with all his social conscience, would go out of his way to find time to concern himself with personal arrangements for this old Irish lady in spite of all the other jobs he was doing in the movement, not to mention having to run a business. And when he went to America he brought her back a big new shawl so that at the next meeting in the city hall you saw Kate in the front row with the shawl around her shoulders.

Eventually George retired and left Sheffield to live near Retford near to where he was born and spent the rest of his days there. He used to love to potter about his garden and told me he had the good fortune to come across an old aged pensioner who lived in the village with whom he had made friends and who was a gardener. So George arranged for him to come and do the gardening whenever he wanted — the old man had no garden of his own — and grow whatever he wanted. George paid for the seed, manure and all the rest of it and he and the old man helped themselves to the vegetables which were produced. It was during the war and it gave George a great deal of pleasure and amusement to think that he and the local parson and all the rest of them were working together in these sort of enterprises. In view of his past activities he said that normally speaking he didn't expect any one of these local village big-wigs would have been seen on the same side of the street as him. But because he was living comfortably, as no doubt he was, they were prepared to work hand in glove with one of Sheffield's leading Communists.

Whenever the party nationally was in dire straits I am convinced that Pollitt used to go to George and get contributions from him, which is why I am sure I was instructed that under no circumstances should I approach George for money as Pollitt did not want the embarrassing situation of repeating the request locally. Nevertheless, George was a great contributor and whenever we were in difficulty locally we were able to go and get his help. I remember during the Air Raid Precaution campaign struggling to raise the money needed to pay for the leaflets. So I went to see George to find out what we could afford. His reply was not to "spoil the ship for a hap'worth of tar", and gave me the authority to get what I needed to run the campaign and he would pick up the bill. And in the course of his time George must have contributed thousands of pounds towards the labour movement. In spite of him being a master baker and having his own business, George's proudest possession was his honorary membership of the Bakers Union.

CHAPTER EIGHTEEN

Spanish Civil War

The attacks of Hitler and Mussolini and the support they were giving to Franco made it evident to the whole of the labour movement and liberal forces that it was in fact a rehearsal for the second world war. This was also a belief of the leaders of the Labour party, but through Attlee there developed the principle of non-intervention, where they claimed the best way of dealing with the problem was to leave it alone; no-one should intervene or supply arms to one side or the other. The only flaw in the argument was they knew, and everybody else knew, that Hitler and Mussolini had no intention of agreeing to the principles of non-intervention and that they were already sending arms, equipment, machines and men in support of the leading industrialists, aristocrats and Spanish landowners rebelling against the democratically elected government of that country.

There were conferences held up and down the country in which the Left in the movement, who supported the civil government of Spain, wanted the British and American governments and others to supply Spain with equipment and money to defeat the Franco rebellion, because they could see if they did not it would merely strengthen the hand of the reactionaries in Europe in their further preparations to declare a second world war. Because of these fears the two campaigns for peace and help for the people of Spain became interwoven and grew into tremendous appeals for food, milk, medical aid and so forth, which was collected from the various areas and estates as the political pressure grew. In my view it is one of the shameful periods of the British Labour government that, in spite of all they could see in front of their own eyes, they were prepared to allow the democratic government and the people of Spain to be destroyed, which ended up in nearly fifty years of life under fascism because the world was not prepared to help them. And of course those who supported the politics of non-intervention at that time bear a certain amount of responsibility for what happened later in the world war. Because if the democratic government had been able to win and defeat Franco, Hitler and Mussolini, who knows what the development of the world would have been without the second world war.

Around this time Tommy Degnam, who was a friend of mine, went to Spain to fight against the Franco rebels but was wounded through a bullet in his lung. He never had it removed but eventually recuperated and was given the job of operating from the C.P. office in Sheffield to get people into the International Brigade. To go to Spain was illegal because of the non-intervention policy. So we had to get them over there in an illegal fashion. The question of who should be allowed to go was not too difficult but you had to make sure that they knew and understood what the issue was about and that they were prepared to take the risks involved. So Tommy and I used to regularly interview young men who contacted us or who were sent to us, to see whether or not they would be prepared to be reasonable supporters and play an active role in the International Brigade. Having helped them make their decision we would usually then put them on the Thursday evening train to London where they would be met and taken to Paris, filtered over the Pyrenees by the Spanish people to the border of Spain and eventually arrive ready for action.

One week, for some reason which I cannot remember, we had to alter our plans and collect the lads together on Wednesday instead of the Thursday. So on the Thursday Tommy and I were sitting in the office when all of a sudden there was a screeching of cars pulling up outside and, like in the American films, the pounding of feet up the stairs before the doors were flung open and in rushed a hoard of police. They looked around and seemed astonished and surprised that there were only two of us sitting comfortably on our own. We asked them what they wanted and what they were doing, and they were very obviously embarrassed and uncomfortable. One of them claimed someone had 'phoned them to say someone was breaking into the office, to which Tommy replied: "That's true enough, you buggers have broken in". They eventually covered their embarrassment and cleared off, but it was obvious that they had been tipped off about our operation but through our by chance change of plans we had managed to foil them.

Working in Sheffield as organiser not only gave me a wonderful experience of working in the wide labour movement in a historic political period but it also gave me the opportunity of meeting and working with a large selection of people who widened my knowledge of human nature and human ability. A number of them had an influence on my development and attitudes, some of whom I have already mentioned. One of these was George Allison, a larger than life personality who was district organiser at the same time as me in Sheffield.

George was a rough broad Scotman always full of fun and if you thought life's difficulties were getting you down you only had to poke your head into his bob hole and George would soon pick you up and show you how everything was worth while. He was enormous fun to work with and I considered it a fortunate experience that I had got him next door. To listen to him joke and laugh you would never think he had any problems but in fact he suffered greatly with his health. Every morning he would get up and have a breakfast of four or five cups of strong tea and four or five full strength Capstan cigarettes. He never ate and had a very bad chest, initially brought about when he went to India in the late '20s on behalf of the International labour movement to organise the Indian trade unions there. He was arrested by the British Raj who held what became known as the Meerut trial where a number of Indian trade union leaders and British people who had become part of the movement there were sent to prison. Before he went to jail he was a 14 stone stocky man with broad shoulders built like a rugby player. When he was finally released he weighed just eight stones and was never able to really recover his health. He went to jail again in 1931 for helping to organise the Invergordon mutiny, so he was a man with wide experience in the working class movement who understood what the battle was for and who, without bitterness, was satisfied with whatever role he could play in organising the working class.

I met him later in 1956 when he called and stayed with us on his way to the TUC congress, because by that time he was the CP industrial organiser. Unfortunately he was taken ill there and had to go home, but never recovered and died at the age of fifty-six. It was one of the first experiences I had had of someone I had been close to dying and his passing had a tremendous effect on me. His wife said that even when he was very, very ill and realised he was not going to get better he made all the arrangements for his funeral "to make sure all the buggers turned out".

Another Scotman I got to know was Jock McCann. He was unemployed and used to come into the office everyday and was a general dogsbody. He would sweep up, act as caretaker and run all the errands, such as selling pamphlets and go collecting around the pubs. Such people are the salt of the earth to the labour movement. They don't want any positions, they don't want to stand for council. Their sole concern is how they can help develop the movement in what little way they can. Jock had a typical working class sense of humour and was an expert when it came to riding the system. For example as the country started preparing for war it got the unemployed to build the air raid shelters. Jock always declared he would be the last to be put to work, so when the Labour Exchange asked him if he was any good with a pick and shovel he replied: "No, mester, but I'm mighty handy with a knife and fork". Similarly, when he won some money on the football pools and got hauled before the court for failing to disclose it while getting benefit he told the magistrates that he had been part of a syndicate of ten and the money had been shared between them all. When the magistrates asked who the other nine were Jock said his loyalty prevented him from disclosing their names. So he got a week in prison. I told him how I admired him for sticking to his principles and not disclosing who the others were, to which he replied: "That was easy, they were nine other bloody Jock McCanns".

When war broke out, though, Jock had to go back into the construction industry which proved to be the death of him as he fell from a staging which broke him up and left him ill for about a year before he died. Over the years most of his activities and meetings had been centred around Barker's Pool where he wandered about for most of his life. So before he died he left instructions with his widow that he wanted his ashes scattered in Barker's Pool during a meeting so he could be there. In spite of great difficulties we managed to persuade some comrades to do just that. A meeting was called and during it one of the women scattered Jock's ashes all around and said that no-one would mind as they would just think she was feeding the pigeons.

CHAPTER NINETEEN

Wartime Wedding

I first met my wife, Beryl, when one day she walked into the office to ask about joining the party, and presumably my explanation and persuasion was sufficient that she not only joined the Communist party but ultimately joined me. I was twenty-nine and we were married within the year.

Beryl comes from a working class family in Sheffield with a long association within the labour and trade union movement. Her mother, in particular, was connected with the Labour party and took part in all the election canvassing and was a regular attender at the monthly meetings of the Labour council where she used to go and sit in the gallery and listen to the meetings and speeches. Beryl's brother was a brilliant scholar and won a scholarship to Oxford. But in the '30s even with a degree you couldn't find work. So he and some other lads of his age in a similar position used to meet at each others homes to discuss and debate issues of the day, and they became heavily involved in the campaign to win political support for Spain.

About this time the Left Book Club was developed and launched in Sheffield by the publisher Victor Gollanze in which a book was published each month on some of the social or political problems of the day, and Beryl played a leading part in helping to develop the Sheffield organisation. They used to meet regularly to discuss the book of the month and, because they were like-minded people of a Left character, they used to also get together for social and other activities. For example the support for Spain in Sheffield produced a very lively organisation which ran cycling and rambling clubs as well as political meetings. Eventually they set up their own Left Club in premises on West Bars which had a big room with a dance floor and kitchen where they served coffee and cakes. It became a thriving organisation and most of the left-wing movement used the premises. At the weekend it was common for a meeting with a speaker to be held on a Friday evening, on Saturday night invariably they had a social with performances by a Left theatre group which they had formed, while on Sundays they usually went rambling in Derbyshire. Beryl graphically recalls the fact that when the CP was asking if they could turn out on a Sunday morning for literature and pamphlet sales and George Allison asked her if she would be there, she said no because they had fixed up a ramble. Apparently George reared himself up and said: "On the day of the bloody revolution we shall find the Red Left book club are out in the wilds of Derbyshire having a bloody ramble". But it developed into a very important organisation in so much as it welded together the various strands of the Left movement and you had a contact point.

We were married on Boxing Day in 1939 and afterwards sent Beryl's family a telegram announcing our news. By that time her parents had split up and her brother had got a job in the civil service in Edinburgh, so the rest of the family had moved there. But Beryl decided to stay in Sheffield, presumably because I was there, and lived with friends while I was in lodgings. By now I had left my job as organiser and gone back into industry so at least there was more chance of us not starving to death. Nevertheless marriage was a dramatic step to take because we had nowhere to live or any furniture.

At that time we had some connections with the Czecholslovakian refugees who were living in Rustlings Road at the bottom of Eccleshall. So when we got married two of our friends there came with us to the registry office. I have always been intrigued about how serious these wedding vows are because it was the first Christmas of the war when presumably nearly every family had got someone who wanted to get married. Because of the numbers involved, the registrar and his staff put two couples in one cubicle and had cubicles all around the place of people waiting to get married. One bloke would come in and read a bit out of the wedding ceremony, then the next bloke came in and did his bit with the ring and then another bloke came and signed you up. There must have been twenty or thirty couples all being dealt with at one time on this conveyor belt system, and I can't help but wonder if it made any difference to our so-called vows. Afterwards we went across to a little hotel, had a bit of lunch with a menu restricted even at that stage by war-time shortages, and spent the rest of the day among the Czech refugees who put on a meal and wedding feast for us. We ate traditional Czech food and celebrated for the rest of the day. The next day Beryl went to work and back to her lodgings and I went to work and back to my lodgings. And that's how we started married life.

But we soon had a stroke of luck, for some friends who lived in a new Bradfield Road flat in Hillsborough offered to lend it to us for a weekend while they were away. While we were there we discovered there were a good number of flats vacant because people were scared of the possibility of being bombed and so had moved out into Derbyshire. So we went to see the caretaker and despite the housing shortages of that time, he gave us a handful of keys of flats for us to look at and pick which one we wanted. So we got our first home.

As I said earlier, I now had a job in industry at the Sheepbridge Stokes works in Chesterfield, while Beryl worked in a dress shop in the centre of Sheffield. I worked a fortnights about shift system, which meant I would spend a fortnight on nights and then two weeks on days and so on. Each shift was twelve hours, so on nights I used to set off from Hillsborough about five-thirty in the evening to catch the six o'clock bus, by which time Beryl had not yet arrived home. By the time I got back in the morning it was about nine and Beryl had already left for work. So during these periods we used to communicate with notes which we left for each other on the table. It is a wonder with such an austere start we ever survived, but we did. When I was on days it wasn't much better because I used to set off for work at about five-thirty in the morning and often used to finish work and go on to a trade union meeting in Chesterfield, which meant I eventually got home about eleven-thirty at night, by which time I was too tired to eat or drink and all I could think about was going to bed. And because of the war we were working seven days a week on long shifts. When I look back I wonder how we managed. Home became a place where I called in sometimes to drop fast asleep, and because of all the stresses and strains of being in the movement it is absolutely clear that if you have not got a partner who knew why this was necessary then obviously not many marriages could possibly succeed.

So I have been very fortunate in the sense I got someone who understands and was able to help and give support and sustain me on the occasions when I was in the dumps wondering what it was all about and if it was all worth while. Not only would Beryl help me to get going again but I was able to discuss political problems with her to help justify the line and policy I was taking. It is terrifically important for anyone who is active in the movement to be married to someone who understands what the thing is all about, what the movement is trying to do and what you are trying to do, because the sacrifices that have to be made are not mere rhetoric they are very real. You have got to be determined about the principles which you joined the movement for and for which you are fighting because sometimes it restricts your activities in other spheres and is a testing time of your own strengths and weaknesses.

Fortunately I have always had the benefit of being married to somebody who understood all the problems and in spite of our fleeting moments together we ended up having four daughters, the first of whom, Janet, was born in 1943, followed by Susan two years later and Mary three years after that. Kate was an after thought and came along in 1955 and Beryl literally brought up the family single handed. Yet our life together has been a co-operative effort and if at any time it is felt that I have done or achieved any success in advancing the movement, then without any question or reservation I'm absolutely certain that at least half the recognition belongs to Beryl because without her it would not have been possible.

CHAPTER TWENTY

Political Splits and Prejudices at the Outbreak of War

With the outbreak of war in September 1939 there became one of the most dramatic periods within the history of the Communist party in Britain. We have to remember that throughout the '30s the CP and left-wing labour movement had been in the forefront of the anti-fascist movement. Wherever supporters of fascism appeared, whether throught the guise of the Mosley black shirt movement or in other forms the Communist party, along with others, organised campaigns to defeat them. This was because although the full horror of the concentration camps was not yet known, it was clear that under Hitler the working class and labour and trade union movement in Germany would be repressed. So there was a tremendous campaign in Britain to awaken the people against fascism.

We fought for policies to build alliances to prevent the advance of Hitler and for a joint British, French, Soviet pact to guarantee the defence of Poland. The campaign failed because one of the factors was the signing of the Soviet-German pact which was a bitter blow to the movement, but which was accepted by the Left as being necessary to defend the Soviet Union because of the attitude of the western governments. Poland's insistence that she would never allow Soviet troups on her soil made a campaign to defend Poland difficult, while the West was obviously not prepared to contemplate any serious build up of an alliance against Hitler.

Amid all this activity there was a leading journalist who used to work for the Times called Frank Pitcairn who joined the Daily Worker as its foreign correspondent. He also founded and sent out a sort of weekly bulletin called The Week which exposed the activities of the upper-class and the undercover diplomatic moves which were being made. Because of his connections with The Times and the fact that he came from a well known family who knew all these top people, Frank was able to make revealing statements about the attempts to mediate and sell-out to Hitler. One day he wrote saying he wanted to come to Sheffield to meet trade unionists and see the background of the working class attitudes, and I had the job of taking him around.

He was a tall gangling man and one of the peculiarities that I noticed was that while he was a brilliant writer and could put all sorts of ideas and information down on paper, when it came to putting it in words on a public platform the brilliance disappeared. This became evident after we organised a big meeting in the city hall for him, and while the information was good in no sense was he a good orator. It is a common weakness that I have discovered throughout my experiences that people who can write brilliantly are generally not good speakers. I suppose it can work on the other hand too as there are good platform speakers who cannot write well. The art of public speaking is to be able to think on your feet.

When war broke out the Communist party characterised it as anti-fascist which meant we mobilised support for it. But a few weeks later the Soviet Communist International decided the war was of an imperialist nature and should be therefore opposed, based on the fact that the western powers and Germany were both striving for supremacy with the ultimate aim of destroying the Soviet Union. The majority of the British Communist party accepted this change of policy but Harry Pollitt opposed it and as a consequence was removed from his position of General Secretary. The split in the movement was real and deep. While I remained a party supporter I remember that when the following national congress arrived a number of us made sure that Pollitt was nominated for the executive committee and that when his name was put forward he got a standing ovation, which was done. But we were reprimanded by the executive of that time, who indicated it recognised that it was in fact an undercover way of declaring our opposition to the political line.

During this period there developed a strategy to turn the issue into a people's war in defence of democratic rights or the defence of people's working conditions and wages. A movement called the People's Convention was formed by a large number of those on the Left led and chaired by D.N. Pritt, K.C., a leading Labour party lawyer, which developed into a real mass movement. Nationally, the Labour party was participating in the national government in which Attlee was Vice-Premier, Ernest Bevan Minister of Labour and Herbert Morrison in charge of the Home Office. And it was while Morrison was in office that the Daily Worker was banned. So the whole of this period was a really traumatic experience in the history of the British working class movement when their resources and abilities were divided.

The whole political situation changed, though, when the Soviet Union was attacked. It then became obvious that the real political aim was the defeat of fascism and everything was to be supported for an allied victory over Hitler. I remember a comment Pollitt made while addressing a meeting at Sheffield City Hall during this build up of war. He looked at the audience before him and said they were better fed, better dressed and looked more prosperous than at any other meeting he had seen there because people now had jobs. And he said it was a reflection on the morality of the society in which we lived that the only time we could provide a decent standard of living for people was as we prepared for war.

Already the factory which I was working at was on overtime. And I recall having been in the job for about two or three weeks when one day the General Manager sent for me. Now this old chap was completely new to me and when I got there he asked me where I had come from and why I had come for a job there. Then he said that he had had a message from the Sheffield police telling him I was a very dangerous character and that it was likely I had got myself set on there so I could blow up the place. So I assured him that nothing I had ever done or would want to do would lead me to do such a stupid thing, and that I was most definitely not in the business of destroying anything. I believe this is one of the fortunate times in my life when religion came to my aid because he was apparently a staunch supporter of the church,and said he had always been brought up to believe that in Britain all men were innocent until proved guilty. Therefore he was going to give me the benefit of the doubt and would do nothing except refuse to allow me to work nights. This was because there was more supervision in the day time and so people could keep their eye on me to make sure I didn't bring in bombs and blow up the place. The fact that to stay on days was a perk which most people fought for and here it was being forced on me was a situation which I thought very humourous. So I willingly agreed to his terms. The bitter pill came six months later when, in order to demonstrate and prove my own integrity, I had to insist I went on nights, otherwise they would say the only reason nothing had happened was because I had been on days. So I ended up arguing these special restrictions which I didn't really want to change as it had left me free to go to my meetings in the evenings. However, it is significant that my first entry into the firm was on this trial or probation basis and that ultimately I stopped there for thirty-eight years.

CHAPTER TWENTY ONE

Wartime Conditions in Industry

The war years were a period when the ordinary working people released all their talents, energy and enthusiasm in the conviction that they were working for a common aim and for the benefit of everybody, and it proved to me that when workers hold these beliefs then they can become all powerful. Consequently it was also the period when the trade union movement grew and developed tremendously, and proved that workers cannot only run industry but that they can do so a damn sight better than those in management.

Because of the constant demands for increased production for the war effort, we set about utilising the trade union organisation and political activities wherever possible in the factories, and set up joint production committees to improve output and supply materials to the forces. This was repeated not only in many factories up and down the country but also in towns where you had local and national committee. I remember in the national shop stewards movement we got together shop stewards representatives from thousands of committees all over the country and held two big conferences in London to discuss how output could be improved and, although you cannot be too simplistic about these things, it was generally achieved through improved organisation and the sweeping away of bureaucracy by putting trust in people who were on the job doing the work. There was the case of Dai Lee, who I have already mentioned, who ultimately became the General Secretary of the Nottinghamshire miners but who had been unemployed up until the war. When the war came he went back into industry and because of his organisation and drive and ability to convince people of the necessity of putting their best in to the job, they built a factory in record time and he was presented with a medal from the government for his efforts. This was a fellow who all through his life had been regarded as a rebel in society but within this sort of atmosphere his talents for organisation proved very useful.

Within the factories there were obviously enormous strains and pressures. I would start the day shift at seven-thirty on Sunday morning and work until the fortnight on the Saturday morning then go on to nights. The only break I had in two weeks was from seven-thirty Saturday morning until seven-thirty Sunday morning. And this was working in factories which were blacked out, with very little ventilation, and with all the shortages and rationings that there were. At Sheepbridge we were producing liners for internal combustion engines for the Merlin aircraft engine which was used in a number of the British aircraft, noteably the Spitfire. We were doing the work on sub-contract for Rolls Royce and on one occasion the representatives from Rolls Royce came to see what more resources or materials they could get because there was a tremendous drive to build more aeroplanes. They were in a panic and wanted to know if the management could improve production to possibly double the number. The management said it was a complete

**In the tool room at Sheepbridge taken in early 1950s.
I'm on the right with my pipe standing beside a couple of workmates.**

impossibility, but sent for me to ask for my comments on the matter. I suggested that rather than take an immediate decision we should invite workers from each particular section which had a part to do and ask them to investigate what could be done in their section to improve output, and then get together to determine on a figure which could be produced. This was a revolutionary idea because it meant that workers were actually determining what the factors were, and ultimately it was decided that if everybody worked together it would be possible to reach the target of 2,000 units a week. It was done, of course, with the built-in safeguard that it would not be taken as a criterion for fixing prices and wages for other jobs and that our piece prices would not be cut. But the men believed that they could achieve what the management believed was an impossibility.

First of all we had meetings in the canteen to explain to everybody what was happening and had articles detailing the matter in the wall newspaper which we produced. Then in each shop we erected a big target board which was hung from the centre main girder and ran from seven-thirty Sunday morning until seven-thirty on the following Saturday night. And each day the figure each section had achieved would be written up, while in the last column was the number which had passed final inspection. It built up an atmosphere that I have never seen in a factory either before or since where, literally, all the people who were working on the shop floor became obsessively interested in how the number was developing and on the last shift of the week, at about two or three on Sunday morning, the man in charge of the inspection department would go up on to the target board and write the number 2,000. It was an incredible achievement and every single person in that machine shop would hammer and rattle in celebration that they had reached target.

It proved to me, and stood me in good stead for the rest of my activities in the trade union movement, that every effort and every step has always got to be taken to inform the people of what you are doing and what is wanted. At one stage it was said that in our factory we had more meetings than they had at the House of Commons, which was probably true because at every step we called a dinner time meeting in the canteen where we discussed the issues with the people. There may have been opposition but the point was that when you had the majority agreeing on a line of policy to follow, the fact that the minority had had the chance to put their point of view and had not been successful meant that at least you had the authority to push ahead with your plans. We deveoped war time newspapers which were a collage of material plus our own articles about the developments, and we were equally able to deal with the problems of the factory. For instance this was a time when women had come into the industry and the law allowed them to work nights only if the rest of the workforce agreed. So we held a ballot, but in order for them to work shifts which suited them better, we introduced three new shifts which ran from seven-thirty in the morning until two in the afternoon, two until ten at night and ten to seven-thirty the next morning, with proportionate payments made to equalise everything out. The old shift had been two in the afternoon until ten in the evening and then until six in the morning, and in my view replacing it helped to solve a lot of problems.

We also joined together with other factories and had joint production committees which combined the various firms, particularly in the engineering industry. The government set up regional productivity committees which had district committees of employees and government representatives, one of which covered north Derbyshire on which I was a representative. We always had to argue to make sure that resources such as electricity and gas were diverted to where they were going to produce the best results. And of course we had all sorts of arguments with people wanting to set up and corner a variety of things for their own private profit, which we had to try and make sure did not happen. One of the amusing things was that they suddenly discovered that all members of this committee were part of the government and that we ought to sign the Official Secrets Act. So I said that as far as I was concerned this was a non starter and I was signing no Official Secrets Act as it indicated that I was not honest or capable of keeping secrets. My integrity was such, I said, that I did not need to sign such a document. They said that was okay but I would have to come off the committee. So I said that if they insisted then I would because I wasn't prepared to sign a secret document which I believed could be utilised to pedal all sorts of complaints. So I never did sign the damn thing, although I think most of the others did, and I was never asked to leave the committee. Which proves that many of these things are done purely as a matter of tradition and have no real purpose.

Probably one of the biggest jobs we ever had to do in relation to organisation involved the canteen, for during a period of serious shortages whatever people could get in a canteen became of uppermost importance in their life. For instance, through the Ministry of Food we would get ration bars of chocolates and the ingenuity people would devise to try to get a bigger share of this chocolate was a thing which amazed me then and has amazed me ever since. If we issued tokens then we would immediately find someone manufacturing tokens, or if we devised a card then we got people forging them. So we decided to use the pay packet and put a special stamp on the back of everybody's envelope in which they received their money as we thought no one would have more than one pay slip. Unfortunately we forgot about the staff in the wages office and we found they were making up empty pay envelopes so they could get extra chocolate. It was this type of thing which, if anything, brought me to despair to think that someone could devise all these ingenious methods for something which was really of no great value. And I don't think it was a problem which we ever did solve. It was similar with clothes rationing where you were issued with a ration book and needed so many tokens for a certain item. Within industry, though, there was some special arrangement — especially for those working in the foundries and castings shops — where they applied directly to the firm. The shop stewards had the job of dealing with these requests and used to hold regular meetings to issue the coupons to people who applied on the grounds that they had burnt their trousers or suffered some similar catastrophe. Because there were no baths at work they used to have to go home in all their dirty clothing so it was largely impossible to get to the truth of the matter. But on the whole we felt we were being conned and probably the wife wanted something, but nevertheless we issued these things as fairly as possible.

Rationing went on for a long time after the war ended and to help us we had an arrangement with the managing director's secretary that we would provide people with notes to hand to her in exchange for coupons. When Stokes was bought out after the war and new management had taken over the secretary sent a message that she was going to come in early one morning and could she see me because it was urgent. When I got there she told me she was leaving because she could not stand working for the new regime and that she had been asked where the coupons were kept. She said she told them that the shop stewards kept them and that I had to take them out of her office because if I didn't the management would take the lot and share them between themselves. And as proof of that sort of attitude she opened a cupboard door and it was full of chocolate biscuits all of which had been allocated to the workforce and should have gone to the canteen but which the management were distributing amongst themselves. She turned to me and said: "The same will happen to your coupons", so I took them, locked them up on the plant and distributed them there. And although we were questioned and quizzed by the management about the coupons we had to say it was our business and they had been allocated to the people on the plant and that was where they were going to stay.

Eventually the canteen was taken over by a private firm, one of many set up during the war to run canteens. When the new people came in they presumably wanted to win some support and respect from the trade union organisations and so collected everybody together to meet the manager and discuss the problems. When we all got there the manager kindly provided us with a mug of tea and a piece of cake and I remember old George Bown declaring that although he was happy to come to the meeting, he was representing the workers and no one was going to buy him over by making him drink tea or eat cake. And he turned to me and said that he was particularly astonished that I would drink and eat and asked how my principles could be squared with this great betrayal of the working class. So I patiently explained that if my integrity was going to be bought by a cup of tea and a cream bun then it was very cheap indeed, and that I could eat cake and drink tea and represent the workers as capably as before. People in the trade union movement fear that people can be bought over by perks, and in some cases there is good reason for it. But if you maintain the principle that you can't be bought then my argument has always been that you must be at least reasonable and sensible about the matter and put your own worth at a sufficient level and make it clear you cannot be bought.

It is a point which I must have made clearly because nearly every foreman at Sheepbridge had at one time been a shop steward. This was because they were people used to living under pressure from their own members and who became articulate and able to understand matters and stand on their own feet. So when management were looking for people to represent them, they automatically went for shop stewards. And I remember jokingly saying to management one day that although I was the longest serving shop steward no one had ever asked me to be foreman. And the reply was that I knew they would not insult me ever by doing that, which was the best commendation I have had.

CHAPTER TWENTY TWO

The Growth of the Trade Unions

When war first broke out there came the anti-Soviet propaganda which was vicious and immense in the sense that everything that was evil was put down to the Soviet Union. But within a few short months there was a complete change in opinion as the Russians joined the war.

As a result all information about the Soviet Union was in high demand, something I particularly noted because as I had been there I was asked to speak to all sorts of meetings, even a Tory women's club in Sheffield. On Sunday nights all over the city the impossible happened when large numbers of working mens clubs halted their proceedings for a quarter of an hour to allow a short statement to be made on the Red Army's progress, followed by a collection for material in support of the soldiers fighting on our side.

The Dean of Canterbury's book The Socialist Sixth of the World, which was an explanation and travel book of the Soviet Union giving his impressions of what was happening in the country and with its people, suddenly became a best seller. It was published at half-a-crown and you could wander around with an armful of books anywhere and sell them all. I particularly remember when he spoke at a meeting in Sheffield City Hall because during the march, which we organised immediately before the meeting, one of the mounted police pulled up and asked to buy a copy of the book, which to me was a revelation of just how far support for the Soviet Union had gone. Organisations of friendship and support for the Soviet Union sprang up everywhere, with even employers organisations utilising the efforts to increase output in every possible way by pretending they were interested in making sure the Russians were supplied with the sinews of war, so that the movement of "Guns and Planes for Joe" became a popular slogan.

At the same time this was the era in which the trade union movement came out of the '30s when in a large number of firms and factories it had been decimated and, in some cases, not even accepted. With the start of the war came this tremendous upsurge of interest in the trade union movement, indicating that not only were workers supporting the ideals and principles of winning the war but at the same time they were demonstrating their own pride and dignity in exercising their power to achieve the trade union movement they wanted. And it suited the purposes of the employers in this new situation and period not only to accept the trade unions but to provide facilities for them and join in joint operations. For if they could harness this tremendous enthusiasm and social consciousness into their own aims of increasing production they were prepared to go along with it.

All firms were experiencing a tremendous influx of labour for everyone was supposed to be either in the forces or in a job, so all sorts of people were brought into industry for the first time. This was one of the reasons why the trade union movement had to recruit and maintain membership to keep some control of these large numbers of people. And because membership expanded rapidly we were constantly having to set up new branches. Some employers decided that if they had to have trade unions then they would ensure they were tame ones. At the Robinsons factory in Chesterfield the first trade union was launched by the management picking two local union organisers then calling a meeting at Bradbury Hall for all their workers who were told they were welcome to join a union and that these two men would lead them. Their aim was that while they were acceding to the new demand from workers to have trade union rights, they were trying to make sure that the negotiations would be on the basis and within the organisation they wanted. And in big plants you would find managements encouraging tame trade union organisations by guaranteeing them sole negotiating rights.

But there were also factories where the trade union organisation had some authority and power and used it in the interest of the people to change whole attitudes. For example at Markham's engineering plant trade union membership had been established for a long time but its strength had never been exercised until the war. Markham was a particular example of the paternalism in industry. In fact, it was always said that if you had your training at Markham's you became one of the best fitters and turners that there were in the district. But this skill that so many of the people there obviously possessed, which was utilised to produce machines of the highest craftsmanship, was never expressed in their wage packets. While they were the better skilled, they were the lowest paid and if they gave twenty-five years service they got the dubious honour of having their photograph hung in the lobby. Only with the onset of war and the development of the shop stewards did the trade union organisation at the plant gain authority and power. And as the shop stewards movement grew factories were able to band together for the first time to discuss common problems and together approach management.

This led to the Amalgamated Union of Engineering workers forming a district committee in Chesterfield to help govern the union on a district basis and bring people into line on the question of wages and conditions, something very necessary at this particular time. Its formation, though, was fraught with quite a number of problems because conditions at the time were hard as most of the people involved were working a seven-day week on twelve hour shifts, and to talk about going to trade union meetings on top of that was very difficult as they were either coming straight from work or left to go onto the night shift. The only full time official was based in Sheffield and he covered the whole area, so if there was a problem at a factory to get him to deal with it was immensely difficult because of the distance and time involved. So the local officials had to try and resolve the matter but often they had difficulty trying to get time off work to get involved in negotiations at some other plant. But we did establish the committee and it has succeeded and survived in so much as we now have a full-time officer of the union in Chesterfield.

The AEU's first full-time District Secretary in Chesterfield was Bill

Mitchell who joined the union at the age of 14 as an apprentice and who remained a member for the rest of his life. He played a leading role in establishing and developing the trade union organisation at Sheepbridge and his organising and negotiating ability, backed by his honesty and integrity, became a by-word recognised by both men and management. Bill was elected to the job in 1973 and remained in the position until he retired in 1986, a year before he sadly died. For much of that time he was also secretary of the town's Trades Union Council and played a great part in establishing its prestige and authority throughout the district, and was one of the founders of the May Day gala and demonstration, which is now the finest in the land. He was also one of my dearest and closest friends and I have never known a man of greater honesty and integrity at any time or anywhere in my life. One of his great passions was the Wortley Hall Holiday and Educational Home, which he saw as a living example of Socialism in practice.

In between times, though, there were some quite amazing characters who took on the job of district secretary, none of whom was a conspicuous success and nearly all of whom had some personal eccentricity which did not improve their efficiencies as district secretaries. This, I believe, was partly due to the arduous nature of the job because as the leading official he was at everyone's beck and call. There was a heavy correspondence to deal with which was done on their own either by writing letters long-hand or by trying to learn to type on an old typewriter, and as their homes were literally district offices there was usually someone calling there most hours of the day and night. On top of this they had to earn their own living while devoting all their own spare time and any other time they could lever out of employers on the "part-time" district secretary job.

An early 1950s May Day group around the Amalgamated Engineering Union banner.

This went on until 1951 when Ron Starling left to take a job in Leeds and the district committee felt it was time to introduce more stable characters. So Eddie Boyce, who was district president, agreed to move over into the secretary's job and I took over his job, temporary caretaker positions until backed by the branches. And it was a partnership which lasted nearly 25 years with due credit going to Eddie for its success. We negotiated with most of the managements in the area at that time but the big difference between then and now was that we could only operate by and large in our own spare time, which meant we had only time to deal with the major issues. This was usually when the stewards had got to the point where they could no longer get agreement, and on reflection I think the fact they had to stand on their own feet and settle their own problems was not a bad thing.

The Ban the Bomb demonstrations were a feature of the early 1960s. This one was taken in 1961 in Chesterfield. Joe Clarke is holding the banner and Eddie Boyce is behind him. I am in front wearing the cap while on my far side is Harry Hicken. In front are Bert Wynn and Tom Swain

I calculate that Eddie and I used to spend at least four nights out of every five on trade union business and activities because the only time we could meet members was when we and they had finished work. In addition we both played an active part in the labour movement, for Eddie was also president of the Constituency Labour party in Chesterfield while I was actively involved in the Communist party in the Sheffield area and, on a number of occasions, fought as a candidate in the local government elections, particularly in the Burngreave ward.

When I look back to those early days I sometimes shudder to recall the effort it took to keep going. Often I would have to travel an hour-and-a-half to go to a meeting before going on to work. I would leave home one day at three-thirty in the afternoon and not arrive back home until nine-thirty the next morning. That feeling of being so tired and weary is one I can still feel to this day. There is no way people can understand what it was like, especially as we were doing most things literally in the dark because of the black-out. My family naturally complained about never seeing me because I was never at home and if I was I was so tired and weary that I used to just sleep. Family life just didn't exist which is why today if there is a choice of being at home or away then I would rather stay at home.

It was dreadful but what kept us going was the tremendous upsurge in the trade union movement. We were now able to go into managers' offices, we were able to go and discuss with employers, we were able to have meetings on the plant, all of which had previously been beyond our wildest dreams. We never thought that the trade union movement in the '30s would reach that position so quickly and the Amalgamated Union was in the forefront because it was the engineering industry which was supplying goods for the war.

There is no doubt that the people who helped establish the trade union movement at that time were heroes who had to grasp the opportunity to establish many of today's accepted practices within industry, such as recognition of shop-floor committees, and it built up a political understanding which laid the basis for future activities of the labour movement that has stood it in good stead ever since.

CHAPTER TWENTY THREE

Picasso and the Peace Conferences

After the war came the development of the cold war with the first anti-Soviet shots being fired by Churchill and others. At the same time the labour and trade union movement developed campaigns around the question of peace, and a number of peace conferences were organised to prevent the re-armament of Germany so that we would never be presented with the sort of horrors that we had been faced within the last war.

One particular conference was against the re-armament of Germany against the cold war and this was held in East Berlin in 1949. At the national conference of shop steward committees within the engineering industry it was agreed to send two delegates to the conference, one of whom was Finlay Hart a boiler-maker and welder from Glasgow, the other of whom was myself. We were given our air tickets but had to cover our own expenses with every day I was away being a day's lost wages.

At that time there was no direct link with East Germany. The only way to get there was to fly from Heathrow to Prague then travel by road from Prague into East Berlin. When we got to Heathrow we were informed the plane had been delayed. So Finlay and I were sitting waiting for our departure when suddenly over the loudspeaker was an announcement asking Mr. Barker and Mr. Hart to go to the controller's office. We looked at each other and wondered what this was about so went to find out what was the matter. They asked us for our passports and looked at the photographs, looked at us, then gave them back to us and said: "It's all right, gentlemen, we just wanted to make sure that it was you who were going". In other words they wanted to register the fact that we were travelling to East Berlin.

When we got to Prague we were met by a car and somewhere along the border between Czechoslovakia and East Germany we stopped to have a meal and while we were there somebody brought me a cigar because they claimed I looked just like Winston Churchill. So being courteous I lit up the cigar and did the Churchill act, and they were so amused that when we left they gave me the rest of the box to take with me.

East Berlin was acres and acres of rubble which they were just starting to re-build. The conference was being held in a hotel which they had just finished building and in which we stayed. But as soon as it was over my financial situation forced me to make my way home again. As I was being driven back to Prague the lad who was driving asked if it would be all right if he called to see his mother in Dresden. I didn't know where it was so obviously agreed, and can still feel the horror of it. Dresden had been bombed to destruction in 1945. Every single building was just a mound of rubble and, from time to time, you would see people come out from cellar steps where they were living. On the journey down we had accidently run over a hare which this young driver was now presenting to his mother with great pride. This was some years after the war yet re-building had not started as they had only just been able to clear the roads. It certainly made a lasting impression on me, and apparently I had not seen it at its worst. I have been to Dresden since and it is amazing to see that they re-built the place into a marvellous and beautiful city.

Shortly afterwards it was decided to hold a second peace conference in Paris the following year. Most trades councils and other organisations were sending delegates to try to build a friendship and association between the East and West. The shop stewards committee asked me to attend, which was endorsed by canteen meetings. Then the Yangtse incident occurred, when a British warship travelling up the Yangtse in China was fired on by the Chinese and held up for quite some time. Eventually the warship scooted down and got away, but there was a tremendous anti-China campaign which affected, by implication, Communists everywhere. The popular press helped drum up the belief that the Chinese had taken our warship and were trying to kill us all, when in fact we were merely trespassing in somebody else's business. So further shop floor meetings were called where some demanded that the peace conference delegation should be cancelled. These meetings were some of the liveliest it has ever been my experience to witness, with people shouting in the canteen and repeating arguments which they had read in their morning papers when generally they did not know what they were really arguing about. However, I managed to persuade the majority to vote to continue to support the conference, and went to Paris.

One of the other delegates in France was the vicar for Darnall in Sheffield, the Reverend Alan Ecclestone, for while the East Berlin peace conference was mainly trade unions, the Paris one attracted a broad range of organisations who all formed part of the build-up of a world-wide movement that supported the idea of peace between East and West. The conference decided that a follow-up one should be held in Sheffield in 1951 organised by the World Peace Council which, by and large, was a combination of the political Left of all religious organisations and trade unionists campaigning for peace and co-operation between the peoples of the world, but particularly between East and West. But the growing number of delegates meant the local organisation committee was presented with enormous problems.

We had booked the Sheffield City Hall for a full week for the actual conference. But there was the big problem of finding accommodation for all the delegates. The damage and destruction which had occurred in Sheffield during the war left the place short of hotel accommodation and those who did have rooms were none too co-operative, having been pressured and influenced by the media campaign which had daubed the conference as an apology for the Soviet Union. So we arranged to use the hospitality of ordinary people who volunteered to provide bed and breakfast. In my own home we had two delegates from Iceland which I considered a particularly pleasant experience as until then I had had no contact with anyone from that country. I was surprised to discover that their organisations were just like ours and that we shared common problems and difficulties.

The first delegates started to arrive about a week before the conference just as the press campaign demanding action from the government became more intense, fuelling every crackpot right-wing organisation in the country to send threatening letters of what they would do to try to disrupt the conference. So security became a real headache as we had some important personalities coming from various countries. Making the necessary arrangements for people to be fed was equally a difficult problem because not everybody believed we could pay, or else refused to help because of their own political prejudices.

Among the number of people who had come early for the conference was the Russian composer Kachachurian, whose music was utilised for the television series the Onedin Line, the French author and writer Henri Barbusse and the world famous painter Picasso. We had meanwhile managed to find one particular cafe and restaurant in the High Street where the manager had expressed support for our aims and agreed to keep a room where we could take VIPs to have a meal, which would later be charged to the conference organisers. Amidst all the welter of those who were not prepared to help this was indeed a bright spot.

So on the Saturday before the conference was due to open on the Sunday or Monday I took this group of people down to the restaurant for a meal. And during the course of the meal Picasso, who could also speak a few words of French and English, took up the menu card and drew his dove of peace which was being used by the peace movement world wide, and wrote a word of greetings on it before signing it and giving it to me. The restaurant manager saw this and later asked me if I thought I could get one for him. Of course I did not think this was possible because you can't just turn to Picasso and ask him to keep doing these drawings. But because I was so grateful that he had allowed us to use the restaurant I said: "Don't bother about asking for another, I'll give you this one". And so I gave him it.

Even now, whenever I relate the story within her hearing, Beryl will play hell with me for being so stupid and accuses me of making just one sacrifice too many for the movement. Whatever the man did with the drawing I have no idea for after the peace conference I never met him again. So I don't know if he realised what he had got and if he ever did anything with it.

By now the press had reached a point of hysteria, screaming about reds at this conference and demanding Parliament ban it. Eventually Attlee, who was Prime Minister at the time, announced that the government had decided it was not prepared to allow people into the country to attend, thus virtually banning the conference. He made some remark to the effect that why anyone should want to go to Sheffield of all places was completely beyond him. In view of the record of the labour movement in Sheffield and the achievements of the labour movement generally it speaks eloquently about Attlee's commitment to it. But this was a Labour government prepared to respond to the demand of the right-wing reactionaries who were in effect acting on behalf of world reaction to make sure that the conference to try and develop the campaign for peace was banned, not through argument but by the crudest possible methods of repression.

While some delegates were already in Sheffield large numbers were being turned back at the ports and it was obvious that we were not going to be able to have an effective congress in Sheffield. So on the Saturday the World Peace Council met in London and the Polish government offered to hold it in Warsaw, and it was agreed to move the venue there. The difficulty was getting those delegates already in Sheffield, and those who had been turned back and who were now spread all over the place, gathered together in Warsaw. So the Polish government provided a passenger liner which docked in London and transferred all the delegates to Poland. Delegates were helped with expenses to London and the journey to Poland cost nothing, but for the trade union delegates it meant three weeks off work instead of one, so I didn't join them. But the Peace Ship, as it was called, did leave for Poland and the peace conference was eventually held there. It suffered in so much as a number of delegates who should have attended did not get there, but by and large it was successful while the Sheffield conference became "the biggest congress that was never held".

The banning added an extra dimension to the developing cold war and deepened the split between East and West with the peace movement suffering a set back, the responsibility for which lay largely with the British Labour government. So embittered were they in their attitude towards the progressive movement that they even preferred to use the forces of state to defeat the aims that the peace movement was attempting to achieve. It is a contribution that should be to the eternal shame of the labour movement.

CHAPTER TWENTY FOUR

Post-war and New Management at Sheepbridge

With the end of the war the trade union movement faced a difficult situation. There had been a great expansion in factory building and employees to cope with the demand for munitions and war work. When the orders finished the workers were no longer needed. There was no question of redeundancy payments, just straight forward notices and the arguments of what to do about them.

Two particular groups of workers had especially benefited from war work; women and disabled people. There had been a tremendous influx of women into the plant doing all sorts of machine jobs and within the engineering industry we always argued that if women were doing the work, in some cases better than the men, as a trade union we should be demanding they be paid the same rates instead of the low pay they were getting. This was very difficult because nationally it was not an accepted practice, just as when the war finished the women were expected to leave the factory first. Although we tried to discuss the matter and deal with the problem on its merits, a large number of women who had come into the factory did in fact leave.

With the drive to get everybody into work a number of disabled, particularly blind, people were also given jobs. This was very interesting because we were asked to find machine jobs which the blind could do. We had a training officer for the blind employed by the Blind Institute who came around and checked up and indicated where he felt blind people could work a machine. To many it was an astonishing thing to imagine a blind person working in a machine shop. But we agreed to try it out and it worked very well. It was an interesting experience because we co-operated with the training officer and discussed it with the people on the shop floor, and I believe it was one of the good experiences in life. They felt they could help and were prepared to accept these people as fellow workmates and make the necessary special arrangements.

For instance those who lived near would call for a blind worker and travel on the bus together, which demonstrated the genuine goodness of the people who were doing it for no other reason than to help. The blind workers soon learned how to use the machines but if they were in trouble we had a special light on the machine and when it was on any one of the people who worked around them would go and see what they wanted. It was a heart-warming experience to see them integrated into the workforce and made welcome, and I am certain they also enjoyed the experience. Yet some jobs blind people may have been expected to easily adapt to turned out to be quite unsuitable. The training officer told us a story which illustrated how blind people have different physiological requirements from others. During the war there was a tremendous demand for photographic film for aircrafts and other purposes and Kodak had asked for some blind people for its dark room, thinking it would be an ideal job for the blind. So the Institute trained some people and took them in but every one of the blind people had to come out because they couldn't stand working in the dark. Which is an example of how normal circumstances do not always apply.

But as the orders were withdrawn the shop floor was gradually reduced and many of these specialised machines and workers had to be laid off, although some who agreed to re-train were kept on. But Sheepbridge Stokes and the shop floor committee had a reputation as a progressive and active organisation mainly because of its strong shop floor committee and the willingness of the management who, at that time, had got people in it who were connected with the Labour movement. And together they were able to sort out many of the post-war problems.

Then in 1949 Sheepbridge, which owned Sheepbridge Castings at Mansfield and Sutton-in-Ashfield and Sheepbridge Stokes in Chesterfield, decided to pull out and sell the business, which was bought by Automotive Ltd. who had a number of other firms up and down the country manufacturing components for the motor industry, and they named the company Sheepbridge Engineering. Now that the steel industry had been nationalised the new company took on the engineering part of the old Sheepbridge Coal and Iron Company and all the engineering section was embraced, along with the other subsidiaries throughout the country, into Sheepbridge Engineering.

With the new company came a new management team, for presumably the trade union activities and reputation had spread into the employers side of the industry. The new managing director was a man called Tom Brown who had been employed in the Morris motorcar industry and it was said that his brief was to smash the trade union movement, clear out the Reds and dismiss any or all of the managers who might be sympathetic to the shop floor. He brought with him the cut-throat principles of management from the motor industry and the crazy personnel system of denoting priority in the pecking or managerial order by whether you were allowed to have a carpet or curtains in your office, and what colour they were. It is claimed that on his arrival at Sheepbridge Tom Brown got all the leading personalities and foremen together and announced that in ordinary life it was said that God is all powerful. That went for everywhere except at Sheepbridge. At Sheepbridge Tom Brown was all powerful and God was second.

He appointed people to management jobs at high salaries and demanded complete subservience. And the penalty for disagreeing was instant dismissal, sometimes at just an hour's notice. His method of management was by terror and the wielding of economic power. It also meant that able men with any pride or dignity would not be prepared to accept jobs under such conditions. So the positions were filled mostly by incompetents and crawlers, who tended to apply the same management principles down the line. The only stop was the shop floor. It gave us an insight into the workings of private industry where on the one hand you had the sheer naked exploitation of economic power where the ability to hire and fire was the major weapon, and on the other the not too sophisticated attempt at paternalism through a sports and social club, annual dinners, trips and gold watches.

It was all part of a programme of softening up the shop stewards and the shop floor which we recognised as management ploys to weaken the trade union movement from its task of defending and improving the wages and conditions of its members. So the shop floor committee faced up to the fact that we were possibly going to have some harder times in defending the aims that we had achieved and the rights and authority of the shop stewards movement. Our attitude was not in direct opposition. We thought the trips to Blackpool and the dinner and watches were all right but should never be considered the alternative to fighting for wages and conditions. We were prepared to accept the pension scheme, even though we didn't feel it was very generous. It operated on the basis you got six old pence — about two-and-a-half new pence — a week for each year of service, but you didn't qualify until you had done twenty years. That meant you got ten shillings, or fifty pence, a week with an extra sixpence for every year after. So if you had done forty years you would have been rewarded with the magnificent sum of a pound a week. Some years later I negotiated an agreement with the management that this pension could be compounded into a lump sum so that whatever amount you would have got in a year was multiplied by eight and men could opt to have this lump sum rather than the weekly pension.

Tom Brown had only been at Sheepbridge a few weeks when one of the foremen in the fettling shop attached to the sand foundry, who was very active outside work with the labour and political movement, was sacked without any rhyme or reason. The lads in the fettling shop immediately took strike action and demanded his re-instatement. We held a meeting of the men that same evening and it was agreed that if management would not withdraw the dismissal notice then strike action would be extended to the rest of the plant. The shop stewards were called into Tom Brown's office who demanded that we resume work, but we said that we had to make the issue clear that as far as his activities on that plant were concerned it had to be done with discussion through the trade union movement or not at all.

He must have thought that we were determined and aggressive enough because within half-an-hour he had withdrawn the dismissal, re-instated the foreman and said that in future he agreed that discussion should take place with the trade union movement before any similar action was taken. To us it was a tremendous victory because there had been fear and trepidation spread throughout the plant at what the new management planned to do, but our immediate response to their action made it possible for us to establish and safeguard our organisation. And we maintained this despite all the blandishment that the management tried to produce.

But others higher up the ladder were removed, and in a very ruthless manner. Managers who did not fit were sent for at a moment's notice and told that their services were no longer required and were given their cards, paid up and told to leave the company car on the way out. One person who had been part and parcel of the development of Sheepbridge Stokes was the technical director Arthur Redfern who helped to develop the whole idea of engine liners and who used to go out to advise people who needed his help. He also acted as a sales representative and was regarded as one of the most popular chaps on the plant.

It is claimed that Tom Brown instructed him to go and get orders from various places and told Arthur to utilise any necessary ploy. If he needed to bribe then bribe as it was his job to get the order and everybody had his price. This was completely foreign to Arthur Redfern's attitude and he told Tom Brown that he couldn't do business like that. So the following week he was sent for in Tom Brown's office and told that they had found he did not fit into their organisation and that he was paid up until the end of the year. He was given his cards and told to be off the plant within the hour. He went back to his office and found the door had been nailed up and all his papers and personal belongings which had been in his desk drawer had been put into a sheet of paper, rolled up and tied in a parcel outside the door. And that was how he was dismissed.

Because he was a popular likeable man we decided to organise a collection in appreciation of his work for the plant and the company. I tried to arrange for one of the foremen or others on their level to do it rather than one of the shop floor people but none of them dared. They said would be more than their job was worth and that they would probably be the next one out. So we did it from the shop floor and booked a pub room in Chesterfield and invited him to come to it. We also invited all the foremen and office staff who had been his work mates over the years but only one dared to come, and he said he didn't want his name mentioned because it would endanger his position.

The management proved itself particularly inept and naive because they were so restricted they did not dare even to think let alone act on their own initiative. The "us" and "them" philosophy was laid down as a major tenet of their attitude to the shop floor; the bosses to rule, the workers to obey. They had no idea who or what workers on the shop floor were like or of the intelligence, pride and dignity of the ordinary worker. They worked on the principle that all shop floor workers were morons without intelligence or interest other than the sheer economic necessity of earning a living. After a life time in industry and having the opportunity of meeting both sides I am firmly of the opinion that the absolute opposite is the truth.

CHAPTER TWENTY FIVE

Shop-floor Development and Extension

Tom Brown was typical of a capitalist representative running private industry. He believed that not only should he have the power to control the workers on the job, but also off the job. These particularly arrogant attitudes were clearly demonstrated by what he believed should be his role in the company. For not only did he see himself as king but that he should have a similarly fitting lifestyle.

The money which was spent on maintaining his own private life style was unbelievable. Hoardes of workmen were taken by lorry — which was nick-named the Amber House special — to work on his private residence. Whatever the whim of him or his family it had to be provided, from houseboats, yachts and swimming pools to a ball of string because someone wanted to tie up a parcel. At work he had a private dining room with staff for his own private use while in his main offices he had the old open fireplace renovated so he could burn pine wood, which he instructed had to be cut into two-inch cubes. Somewhere down south he had a shooting lodge and on one occasion he bought a whole load of reproduction furniture for it, which he had delivered to the works so the joiners could spend their time trying to make this brand new furniture look like antiques. They even went to the lengths of drilling small holes in it to make it look as though it had been attacked by woodworm.

I don't know if these sorts of experiences are common in private industry but I have always said that when the media have been busy exposing the imperfections of nationalised industries they should have turned the same spotlight on to private industry which would have made the nationalised industries look like the paragons of efficiency.

In this sort of situation it was necessary for us to maintain an active strong organisation, not only at Sheepbridge Stokes but in the other works and departments. So the Sheepbridge joint shop stewards committee was established. We also became aware of the other factories within the group and the fact that the management used them against us during negotiations by claiming the other plants either produced more units or goods more cheaply than we did. We didn't believe it but decided we should make contact with the workers in the other plants and attempt to build a joint organisation. This was not easy as some of the factories had no trade union organisation while others had very little.

Through the AEU's machinery we made contact and sent delegations of people down to the southern factories at weekends and arranged to meet up with selected workers to discuss the problem in their own plants. On two occasions we went down on the Saturday, met the people on the Sunday and then I spoke at factory gate meetings on the Monday dinner time and established trade union organisations in those plants and the other subsidiary firms. We eventually got sufficient interest and support to call the first meeting of the Sheepbridge Engineering Combine committee which brought together stewards from the various plants, many of whom were very new.

I recall at the very first meeting overhearing Joe Twiss, who had become the convenor of the foundry section at the Sutton-in-Ashfield factory, talking to the rest of the Sutton stewards and saying he hoped they realised that they had been drawn into a hot bed of Communism. This of course, was a long way from the truth because they were nearly all, bar our own factory, raw recruits. Joe remained a good friend and despite his early comments turned out to be one of the most militant stewards in the combine and despite his tendency to anarchism, played a leading and valuable role in maintaining a combine committee over a number of years. The committee prospered and played a vital role in the building of the trade union movement throughout the Sheepbridge group, defending the wages and conditions of all who worked there irrespective of what or where the particular factory happened to be.

By now it was the mid '50s and the Chesterfield factory was working short time on a three or four-day week. The management complained that they were not getting orders because our prices were too high and they wanted to reduce both prices and manning levels. They claimed that at a factory at one of their subsidiaries in Birmingham, Harold Andrews, they had one man working four machines whereas we had got one man working one machine. So we contacted the stewards at Andrews and arranged for a delegation of four of us to visit the factory the following week. When we got there we contacted the local steward, told him we had arrived and were across the road in the pub, and he came over to see us. We discussed what we wanted to do and ascertained whether we could look at these four machines that were supposedly being worked by one man.

The steward went away to contact the local manager and ask for his permission to show us around the works. Now what tale he told him I do not know but when we got there we were welcomed by the manager and given a guided tour, and I sensed that he thought we were much more official than what we were. And while I kept the manager in conversation I instructed the other lads to go and look at these other machines to find out all they wanted to know, which they did. Of course the story being told in Chesterfield had got no basis on fact at all. In fact we must have been producing the same units at about half the price that they were at Harold Andrews. I do not know if the manager was confused over our delegation but not only did he give us the full run of the factory but then proceeded to take us into the local pub where we were royally wined and dined. Whatever happened when we revealed in negotiations when we got back that we had been and looked at the situation at Harold Andrews and knew very well that it was mere bluff I do not know. Especially when they no doubt discovered that not only had the manager given us all the information we had wanted but paid for our lunch as well!

They never apologised for lying or trying to negotiate by deceit and this was a management, in my experience, who were past masters at this art. They would make one statement one day then refute it the next and then deny that they ever even said it. I recall this occurring in one piece of negotiation when we were being treated as naive idiots. It was obvious they were lying and so we just got up and marched out and said we would only come back when they were prepared to start telling the truth and deal with people and trade unions with the necessary respect that they themselves expected. As I said at the time, in negotiations you can normally, despite your differences, negotiate with anybody. There is always a basis on which negotiations can take place providing you respect the others integrity. But there is one situation which you can never negotiate and that is with liars. That is an impossibility.

There is no doubt that Tom Brown would have liked to have got rid of me at all costs and the only reason I stayed at Sheepbridge was because of the shop floor who made sure that I was protected. To have attempted to get rid of me they assumed would have meant a complete stoppage of the plant which they were not prepared to risk. As convenor I acted on the principle, along with the other shop stewards, that any problem that arose on our factory floor was ours and that in the whole time I was convenor I never had a full-time official on the plant. My view was that if we didn't know and couldn't provide the answer then nobody from outside could. As soon as you started talking about bringing in full-time officials then you begin referring to agreement books, rules, regulations and legislation, and once you get tied up in them your chances diminish with the amount of legalities in which you get entangled. We didn't have anything against full-time officials. We understood that they were constrained to work with a code and set of rules and regulations but we were not. Therefore our attitude was a simple one; we always fought it out there and then. Nobody could then say that we had or had not signed this or that. We were concerned with the reality and issues involved and if we could not solve them then nobody else could because nobody else knew them. And over the years I think that, in general, the management accepted that point of view. No one with any sense, even from the management, could say that our shop stewards committee ever used its considerable amount of power irresponsibly.

During this time Tom Brown operated his annual dinners for foremen, which were amazing events. They decorated the canteen, put up awnings outside and laid down carpets with all the leading customers, managing directors and industrialists attending. And it was the accepted practice that you drank yourself silly. They were complete orgies which apparently pleased the hierarchy no end. It was males-only, of course, and after the dinner speeches would come on the so-called entertainment, which usually meant strippers. This is what they believed was the cultural level of the masses. And as the night wore on Tom Brown used to retire from the main hall up to his private dining room with his cronies and the stripper would go and perform among the more intimate surroundings. To me it just showed their cultural intelligence level and I used to ask what, in God's name, did they either read, think, or do other than their job because in most cases Alf Garnett was an intellectual compared with them.

So the shop stewards committee decided to put on its own dinner. We applied for the use of the canteen and planned to invite all employees and their wives. It was refused and we said we did not understand what was so objectionable about us having a dinner. So eventually I was sent for to the sanctum to see him about it. Going to Tom Brown's office was an amazing experience. It was down a long corridor as though you were walking to an execution. You were then announced and were ushered into a room up to your knees in carpet and then left to sit alone. This is the usual tactic if you want to destroy anyone before you see them. You fill them with awe and trepidation and then leave them in a great big room entirely on their own. Part of the tricks of the trade. So I thought the best thing to do was to light my pipe. After a while Tom Brown opened the door into another great big room and the personnel manager sat on the edge of his seat in obvious and complete terror. Tom Brown was at his desk and first picked up his cigarettes, offered me one, "No thank you", offered me a cigar, "No thank you", and so on, until I turned and said, "If you don't mind I'll continue smoking my pipe". He said that was all right and after a minute added. "I think I'll go and fetch mine. You look too bloody comfortable with that". Which is what he did.

So we sat and discussed the matter of the shop stewards dinner. He wanted to know why we wanted one so I said it would be a social event to which the men could bring their wives. He replied that we could have the canteen for the men but that he didn't agree with wives. So I asked why in God's name not. The very fact that a man is able to bring his wife on a Saturday evening guarantees that the event will proceed with no trouble. A normal man who goes out for a social evening with his wife acts with the kind of responsibility, respect and pride that he has when his wife is with him. His foremen's dinners, I said, had men crawling about on their hands and knees and barking like dogs, with special staff on at the ambulance room to deal with the drunks. Our dinner would not be like that. So eventually he gave the personnel officer permission to grant us the canteen and offered to provide a bottle of beer for the men and a glass of wine for the ladies at each place.

And the shop stewards committee's annual dinner became an established prestige event because we invited the local Member of Parliament, Mayor, leading trade union officials, the manager of the Labour Exchange and all others who were anxious to come. There were no speeches and we used to get up to 400 people there with never the slightest trouble. In fact it became so successful that the management said we could no longer have the canteen. So I asked Robinson and Sons if we could use their Bradbury Hall, they agreed and it became the regular annual venue. Apparently Tom Brown later sent a representative to see if he could hold his foremen's dinners there, but their reputation had spread and they refused to allow him to use it. It was a typical example of the difference of attitudes in life. They honestly believed that all working men preferred to go out on a Saturday on their own and get drunk.

Because the Combine committee needed to raise a good deal of money to finance its activities it was decided to establish a tote fund to pay for trade union and a number of benevolent activities. We issued a prospectus to all the people on the plant indicating what the purpose and use of the money raised would be, which included long term sickness and funeral grants and, at a later date, we used some of the money to establish holidays at Wortley Hall for retired members and to give Christmas grants to all retired people at Sheepbridge. It was also felt that while we were active it would be an advantage if we could get some direct information on the standing of the company itself. So we decided to become shareholders so we could get direct communication from the company and bought 500 shares which entitled us to receive the annual balance sheets and get an invitation to the annual meeting. Although we never actually took up that opportunity we always held it and, during discussions with the management, would say that if we were in any difficulty at any time we would not hesitate to try to utilise the annual meeting to raise whatever problems we had. And in most cases it produced the necessary pressure to get settlements which I am sure we would not have got without being able to use that particular weapon.

Tom Brown eventually retired and, despite having a wife and son, they say he apparently died a lonely man in a hotel room somewhere.

CHAPTER TWENTY SIX

Vin Williams and Wortley Hall

We have mentioned before the fact that Vin Williams was a larger than life character who was always developing ideas for projecting the labour and trade union movement into the future. He was full of madcap notions, often dreaming up something new before finishing the first.

During the General Strike Vin was sent to jail and victimised so had to earn his living in all sorts of ways, such as carting clothes and other items door-to-door around the houses and selling patented medicines. He had this stuff in a bottle which he called "It's It". And whenever anyone asked what it did he used to say: "Well you can either clean carpets with it or take it for a cough". After a while he returned to the pits and became a leading figure amongst the miners. But he was quite a maverick in relation to his trade union activities and at one stage even got expelled from the NUM for leading a sit-down strike during the war at Renishaw and Mosborough colliery. He was the only local person that I knew who received the accolade of the working class movement during the general strike, which was a medal presented by the International Class War Prisoners Aid which existed to honour all sorts of people who had suffered and been part of the battle of the working class.

I remember the time he decided to launch a scheme for the labour movement's football pools which he claimed would put Littlewoods and Vernons out of business. But unfortunately it was the labour movement's pools that went out of business, and created a great deal of difficulty and tragedies among the ordinary working class people who had put their life savings into the scheme before it collapsed. But I always had a soft spot for Vin because he had this boundless enthusiasm for the labour movement and the working class and always believed no matter what scheme he was busy with at that moment that there was no obstacle that could not be overcome.

He was also a very able and capable orator and lecturer and so eventually became a full time lecturer for the National Council Labour College, working primarily in South Yorkshire and North Derbyshire. In 1949 Vin heard that Wortley Hall, a large stately home near Barnsley belonging to the Warncliffe family, was up for sale. So, being of a visionary nature, he immediately saw its potential as a place the movement could use to organise its own weekend schools, educational courses and holidays. He believed Wortley Hall would make the ideal place so he called a meeting of interested people from the labour movement and brought them together on 5th May 1949 to discuss the matter. It was decided that the meeting should constitute the provisional committee with power to act and that as such we should take all the necessary steps to acquire, furnish and equip Wortley Hall as a labour college.

Our first call was to the estate agents when we discovered that due to certain entailments of the property it could not change ownership and so would have to be taken over on the basis of a lease. So we agreed to pay £50 rent for the first year and £500 for each succeeding year, plus rates. This was because Wortley Hall had been left vacant for some considerable time and was very dilapidated. During the war it had been occupied by troops as a sort of camping place and no repairs had been carried out before or since that time. Our main job was to get as many volunteers as possible to the place to try to get it in some sort of order, and during the first year whole gangs of people from all sorts of organisations connected with the labour movement went for working weekends to Wortley Hall. Joiners went to do joinery work, bricklayers laid bricks, electricians repaired the wiring while many more just went along to sweep, scrub and clean — all along with their sleeping bags.

Wortley Hall is still the working class monument it set out to be, with many of the founder members now enjoying its facilities during retirement (I'm on the right at the back).

Then there was the problem of furnishing and heating the place as well as providing all the small necessities such as knives, forks, spoons, bedding and so on. So it was decided to try to raise the money through the labour movement. First of all we appealed to sympathisers to take out shares at one shilling, or five new pence, each. Any shareholder could buy up to 200 shares but no matter how many shares you had you could only have one vote. The executive committee was formed from shareholders who were elected at the annual meeting. These steps were taken so no organisation could buy the place up or get enough shares to control it. It was a method by which the members of Wortley Hall maintained democratic control. Appeals for finance were also made to national trade union organisations but initially we did not get much response, which is why all sorts of schemes were launched to raise money.

One of these was a national prize draw on the St. Leger which raised £1,300, a tremendous amount of money in those days. Another was a national Christmas draw which the executive committee decided to run through Vin Williams in 1951, and Post Office vans were drawing up all day long bringing bags packed with draw tickets. Unfortunately in those days you were not allowed to run draws and raffles on a national basis and when the police were tipped off and raided the place they found all the sacks stacked up waiting to be sorted out. They confiscated all the draw tickets, correspondence and money and then charged the executive committee members of organising the prize draw. Later they appeared before Barnsley magistrates and were fined a nominal sum which the magistrates paid between themselves, so the expression of solidarity over what was being done was pretty well known in the labour movement.

Eventually, by means of getting sympathetic people in business to provide us with equipment, Wortley Hall was opened in May 1951 by Sir Frank Soskice, QC, who was then Labour Member of Parliament for one of the Sheffield constituencies. It was done only through the tremendous amount of activity and support from all sections of the movement where for many more years people still went at weekends to volunteer their labour to enable the place to develop. Because, I believe it is fair to say, in those days when you went to a school or an event at Wortley Hall you went on the principle of sacrifice. It was freezing cold and the plumbing and furnishings left a lot to be desired. But I remember those days with affection because Vin, who sort of lived there, used to go into the main lounge and tell stories of his early pioneering days on speaking tours and so fired them with so much enthusiasm for the movement that they all went to bed warmed through to last them until morning. Nowadays it is peculiar to think that people ask us to turn the heat down because they are too warm, and certainly makes a change from the days when you had to borrow extra blankets and coats and fill a hot water bottle before going to bed. But having got over those days the people who actively took part in them can now walk about with their chest out and say, well I was one of the pioneers who used to come in the old days.

So Vin's vision of a place where the working class movement in its broadest sense could have facilities for a school, eating and entertainment came to fruition. But at the same time he was a man who did not like his ideas cluttered up with practical application of them. So from the outset we were very fortunate to have Bill Robinson, manager of the Sheffield Co-operative bank, as treasurer who helped with the development and financial side of the operation, and Alf and Marion Hague who provided the organisational and practical skills to put Wortley Hall on a proper business footing as well as providing a service to the trade union and labour movement.

The initial lease was for fourteen years with an option of renewal for a further seven years. And after we had been open for some time the committee felt they would like to discuss rent and an extension of the lease. So a delegation went to see the estate agents who suggested that instead we bought the property because the restrictions on ownership had now been lifted. So it was agreed that we buy the hall with twenty six acres of grounds and four cottages for ten thousand pounds. Its value for insurance purposes, at the time of writing, is two million pounds. But people must remember that if we had not put all the work in then in no way could they have sold it to anyone else. For the organisation it was a very good buy because everything that has been put in it has added value to the hall.

I have been connected with Wortley Hall from its very conception and this aspect of belonging to it is an aspect that has pervaded the whole of the scheme from its beginning. If I am speaking to residents who are there for a holiday I always say that as soon as I go through the door I feel that I am at home, and it is a feeling which expresses itself all the time. It has only been achieved because ultimately we were able to win the support of the trade union movement which is visibly recognised in many of the rooms. For instance the lounge has been financed and furnished by the Amalgamated Union of Engineering Workers, the dining room has been done by the Foundry Workers, the television room by the Electrical and Technician's Union, the small dining room by the Fire Brigade Union and the library by the Yorkshire miners. It has developed into an organisation that most trade unions, including the Trades Union Congress, use at some time or other.

It is still run by the executive committee and you still have to be a shareholder to be on it, and until recently that caused us some problems. The original register had to close sometime around 1956 so to find people who had got shares became increasingly difficult as they slowly died off. Then there was the problem that to send out a notice of the annual general meeting cost more than the shilling share. So in 1983 we called a general meeting through circulation and got an agreement with the registrar to open the share register for three months. The minimum number of shares was 100 for £5 while the maximum was 200 for £10. So now we have a very much wider and younger group of people who are shareholders and eligible to be elected onto the executive committee, safeguarding its future to some extent.

We also have something of very great value to the movement. Anybody who goes to experience a holiday or weekend school there may think that they have come to some sort of oasis of Socialism, but we wanted to make sure that Wortley Hall was not merely utilised as an escape from the everyday activities of the movement but a place for those in need of refreshment and the reviving of the faith. All those connected with it through the years want it to be used so people can go back and participate in the movement with even greater strength and enthusiasm than before they arrived. In my view I think we can claim it to be a tremendous success and a statement of what, given the will and enthusiasm of the working class movement, can be achieved. Wortley Hall proved there is no obstacle that they cannot overcome provided there is the determination to do it. How ever it develops in the future it can be regarded as a monumental success to the socialist spirit of a large number of dedicated people.

Tragically Vin, the man who first conceived the whole idea, broke all connections with Wortley Hall due to an unfortunate misunderstanding. When we needed to organise an overdraft to pay for furniture it was disclosed that Vin, through one of his previous transactions, was an undischarged bankrupt and therefore there was no possibility of him being able to get involved with the finances of the operation. This upset him terribly because I imagine he believed his own integrity was being questioned, and it is said he went and collected his little typewriter and his jacket and walked out and never went back again. I believe it was only Vin's vision and spirit to enthuse others to give up weekends and holidays to work on a derelict building and its grounds that enabled Wortley Hall ever to become a reality. I am only sad that as it was beginning to become established due to his work he decided to break the connection and it is a thousand pities that he never lived to see it blossom as it is now.

CHAPTER TWENTY SEVEN

Communist Parliamentary Candidate for Chesterfield, 1951

In the 1951 general election the Communist party decided to put up 52 candidates to try and make some impression on the election scene. And because of my connections with the industrial and trade union movement in Chesterfield I was asked to be the party's parliamentary candidate for the town.

Up until then I had fought as a candidate in the local government elections in the Sheffield area on a number of occasions, particularly in the Burngreave ward. And it was during one of these periods that I met up with one of the best friends I ever had, Fred Hill, who was a secretary of the National Union of Railwaymen, president of the Sheffield and Chesterfield district committee and who later sat on the executive committee. He was a great character who argued that we had walked up and down Burngreave streets canvassing and holding meetings so often and for so long that even the dogs knew who we were, and that we had better make a change before they thought we were fixtures. In later years he always told people that I used to say that if at any time we had done the impossible and won the seat it would have been because we had a first class candidate but if, as normally happened, we lost the election then that was the result of having a bad agent.

I was the first and, up until now, the only Communist party parliamentary candidate to stand in Chesterfield. The Labour candidate was the sitting MP George Benson, the Tory candidate was the Duke of Devonshire — who was then the Marquis of Hartington — and there was a Liberal candidate. George Benson was regarded both in and outside the movement as a right-winger and by many as utterly useless. I remember that just before an earlier election he had been injured in a motor accident and was forced to sit down while addressing a mass meeting. This drew tremendous sympathetic applause from the audience, only spoilt when one cruel individual said he believed that was the most effective speech he had ever made in his life. Nevertheless he was the chosen candidate and consequently I was considered by some to be committing the greatest sin of all by standing against him.

Curiously enough the issues that were then being argued about were very similar to those of the '80s in the sense that it was a question of the government imposing economies to keep the country so called solvent, the need for a campaign for peace and against developing nuclear weapons, and the argument for expanding the economy to improve conditions, wages, social services, housing and so so. The line of the Communist party and generally socialists of the Left was to run the system so as to produce the best for the people. Socialism means in effect the changing of the system with the resources of the country being devoted to the well being of the people. The Labour party's line was basically how to run capitalism better than the capitalists.

My "official" election photograph when I stood for Parliament as the Communist Party candidate in the 1951 elections in Chesterfield.

The campaign was also run on very similar lines to those of today, although I have known an election in Chesterfield when they had only one meeting throughout the whole campaign. One meeting I particularly recall was organised by the Transport and General Workers Union at the St. Helen's pub to which all four candidates were invited to speak. I remember being third in line and obviously bumped into the Tory candidate, the Duke of Devonshire, who proceeded to say how exhausted he was and he did not know how I had the strength to keep going on, to which I replied it was quite easy as I was used to working for my living. I also remember that at most meetings sitting at the back of the room would be a representative from Sheepbridge who had no doubt been instructed to give a faithful report back to the management of what had taken place. At this one particular meeting I spotted two managers and life long Tories who were waiting to see if I said anything in connection with Sheepbridge which they could report back to Tom Brown. You can imagine the embarrassment of these two individuals when we indicated who they were and why they were present, and pointed them out to the rest of the audience. But they did not dare leave for fear of the All Mighty Mr. Brown.

The attitude among the general workers to a Communist party candidate was curious. If I could have translated all the sympathy into votes then it would have been a landslide victory. But there was a great loyalty to the Labour party even if they openly criticised its policies, and it was impossible to get over that barrier. A good number of people used to come up to me and tell me to stand as a Labour candidate where I would have much more chance of winning as people would not have the same number of qualms as they had in voting for the Communist party. The feeling was that they would ultimately vote Labour however much against their will. So there was a good deal of ground swell support but it could not be translated into votes.

It was the same with the media where some said that the best political statements and speakers came from us. One first-class speaker who supported many of my meetings was the Reverend Alan Ecclestone, vicar of Darnall who I had first met at the Paris peace conference. Not only was he a practising vicar but a staunch supporter and member of the Communist party. He was asked how he reconciled that with being a Christian but he said for Communists it was fairly easy. If ever you went to the Darnall rectory it was full of all sorts of homeless families and tramps, and one of his sons, Jake, later became a leading official within the National Union of Journalists. The press also talked a lot about what they coined as "Bas' glamour girls". These were members of the Young Communist League who would support my meetings or else go and torment the Tories. There were quite a number of them who included such people as Betty and Del Vardy, Glenda Wynn and Kath Barlow. Another curious thing about the press was that for years later, and it did not matter what I had done or said, whenever I was reported in the press — particularly in the Derbyshire Times — they used to refer to me in brackets as the Communist Candidate to make sure readers knew just exactly who I was. Their attitude was not unsimilar to the mound of hate letters I got during the campaign, particularly from

Christians who wrote hoping that my wife and children would die in poisoned agony. It is a curious fact that these sorts of Christians always use their faith in the hope that you end up dying a horrible death. It didn't upset me, nor did the returned election addresses with the evil hangman's noose drawn all over them.

In the main we had very good meetings with good attendances and much enthusiasm with reasonable support. You felt you were doing really well up until the last two or three days and then when you went out into the mining areas you sensed a perceptible change of mood in the sense that you saw the traditional Labour people putting up their posters and the Labour vote solidifying. But I am convinced that at least we did raise the issue which the campaign was all about and turned out the Labour voters to vote, but unfortunately not for us.

In the final event I collected 534 votes and lost my deposit. And I recall that as I sat at the back of the Market Hall during the count reading my newspaper a lady, who I now recognise as being the Duchess of Devonshire, came to me and commented on the fact that I was not milling around the table where they were conducting the count and that I did not look to be very interested in the proceedings. To which I replied that was because my political sense meant I already knew the result.

CHAPTER TWENTY EIGHT

Eric Varley and the Benn By-election

When George Benson announced he did not intend to contest the Chesterfield parliamentary seat at the next election in 1964, the activists in the trade union movement saw this as a chance to replace him with someone who would support left-wing and more militant policies.

The constituency had been burdened, and I say that advisedly, for twenty-five years or more by George Benson, an arch apologist of the capitalist system and believer and supporter of Keynes' economic theories, and because the early Labour governments had applied these policies he declared never again would we see a situation where we had unemployment. He was referred to as a financial expert by the local press and pundits but never in my discussions with him could I discern this authority. This may have been due to the fact that by profession he was an estate agent and the family firm used to look after Oswald Mosley's Manchester estates. In parliament his time had neither effect on policies nor did he make any major contributions to the political activity either in the movement or the constituency, and he found himself a comfortable niche as Chairman of the House of Commons Library committee which provided him with accommodation and a private office. So for a number of years if you asked him about any political campaign or the policies that were developing at that time, he would excuse himself by saying that while he agreed with what you were saying he could not do anything about it because he was tied up with the Library.

At the time of his announced retirement Eric Varley was the new rising star within the miners' union. Eric's father, Frank, was an old NUM member and when conscription came along, where you either had to join the army or work in the pits, Eric got a job at the Area Workshops. Up until then he worked as an apprentice turner at Staveley where he became the first Chairman of the Amalgamated Engineering Junior Workers Committee. As a member of the NUM he began attending the Miners' Council where he came under the influence, guidance and patronage of Bert Wynn who was then General Secretary of the Derbyshire Miners. This was the time when Bert was developing a group of young people within the union into future leadership positioning.

This education programme involved regular weekly day classes at the miners offices which, at that time, included Eric Varley, Peter Heathfield, Dennis Skinner, Stan Mellors and a number of others. Bert's idea was that it was not sufficient merely to develop activity within the trade union movement but that you had to also create an effective influence in the political sphere, and he was always working to try to make the NUM a dominant influence within the labour movement in this area. He envisaged a programme in which not only would we maintain Labour representation in parliament but that these representatives would be miners representing the NUM and their interests, particularly in the seats covering Chesterfield,

North East Derbyshire, Belper and Ilkeston. Through the NUM various people, including Eric Varley, were provided with opportunities to get a wider knowledge of the movement. For example Eric participated in delegations to Spain to study the conditions of the miners under Franco and he went to East Germany and participated in various day schools which eventually provided him with the opportunity to attend Ruskin College, Oxford.

Eric Varley (left) taken in 1965 at the annual Sheepbridge shop stewards dinner.

So it was on this basis that Eric Varley was chosen to win the miners nomination for Chesterfield, with the support of the engineering union because of his early connections with it. The campaign itself was most fierce and ruthless. There were quite a number of candidates and people interested in the seat, so it was necessary to do some considerable manoeuvring. I recall the executive committee taking the decision to place an age limit of forty-five on all possible candidates. This was not merely because everyone had suddenly become an ardent supporter of youth in the movement, but because they felt that by imposing the age limit they could eliminate people whose policies they did not like. The NUM was forced to muster all its forces by encouraging people to become individual members of the Labour party so it had the largest possible number of delegates at the selection conference. Without all that mobilsation people agree there is no way Eric Varley could have been adopted as a candidate. In fact of the four candidates — Eric, a man called Bradley who was the Railway Clerks union president, and two local candidates Rolandson and White — it was later said that if the candidate had been chosen purely on charisma and ability to speak then Eric Varley would have been bottom of the poll. But because of the efficiency of the miners mobilising their delegates and the support of the engineering delegates, they were able to swing the ballot so that he was chosen as the left-wing candidate to stand in the following general election.

So on October 15th, 1964 Eric Varley became the parliamentary candidate with the support of the Left and for the Left, in the sense that we expected that once in Parliament we would have a new voice to support left-wing policies. But I believe that when Eric was promoted by Harold Wilson to be his private parliamentary secretary, he knew he faced the choice of either remaining just a constituency MP — and a voice of the Left — or of becoming a Cabinet Minister, and a voice of the government. The two, on this occasion were not compatible and Eric chose the latter and eventually became Industry Minister. Obviously the Left in his constituency felt betrayed, but on the other hand others were delighted to have a Cabinet Minister represent them and put Chesterfield in the national limelight.

I must admit to being completely mystified as to why Eric made the choice he did. He followed an all too familiar path taken by many on the Left before him and no doubt will be followed by many more. Yet I doubt if they got any greater personal satisfaction or contentment from life than I have done. For I can honestly say that I believe that in the end I got far more reward than can be measured by success, money or material objects.

When Eric Varley decided to resign from the House of Commons and enter private industry as Chairman of the Coalite Chemical group I can't say I was very surprised. And immediately there was talk of who was going to be the candidate to follow Varley in the March 1984 by-election. Ironically enough those who were arguing that Chesterfield was a right-wing area and that we needed someone in the model of Eric Varley who was a local man and who knew the constituency were the very same people, in the main, who fought tooth and nail to prevent Eric Varley becoming adopted as the candidate. Once again the left-wing was faced with the problem of battling for the soul of the movement as it had tried to do twenty or so years earlier. And once again those who were against bringing in a progressive candidate were the same people who were now opposing Tony Benn. It was the activists, socialists and trade unionists, those who had kept the faith, who were arguing that here we now had the chance of an excellent candidate by bringing in Tony Benn.

The activity which developed around the adoption of the candidature of Tony Benn was amazing. It released the pent-up feelings of all those in the locality who were committed to socialist ideas who really felt in their bones that they were being given, for the first time, something to fight for and something to get their teeth into for the movement. There was a challenge and they revelled in the battle, despite all the media attention and every

Tony Benn and Labour Leader Neil Kinnock during the 1984 Chesterfield by-election.

artifice used to make sure Tony Benn was defeated — slander, lies and the dirty tricks brigade. The campaign became a revivalist one based on the rejuvenation of the old socialist spirit with comrades and activists coming from all four corners of the country and even abroad to help in the campaign. And it seemed to me that they were enjoying this rejuvenation of spirit of their own particular faith and the basic principles of socialism. They were able to state them and support them without cringing or apology.

There were mass meetings the like of which had never been seen for more than a decade and while it was true there was a good deal of television coverage, the campaign itself was not fought out on the box but at grass roots level in the streets, the factories, the market place, the pubs and the clubs. The issues were taken to the people. Tony Benn, to his eternal credit, faced up to the media and his opponents and declared that socialism was not a dirty word and that its principles were worth fighting for because they were in the interest of the ordinary people. On this basis a campaign was developed on the broadest possible support from the whole of the movement with Right, Centre, Left and trade unionsts all working together. It was the best example of a united movement that has been achieved in any constituency.

Despite all the desperate attempts by the media and opponents a resounding success was achieved. The election campaign provided a firm base for the revitalisation of the constituency party and of the labour movement. Labour party membership increased tremendously, political discussion is the order of the day and in Chesterfield, I think it can be rightly said, there is more genuine political activity embracing the broad movement from right to left than anywhere else in the country. The by-election became a catalyst around which the battle for the principles of socialism were fought and won.

In today's political atmosphere, with discussions around the so-called new realism, it would be well for supporters of the labour movement to recall that the Chesterfield by-election demonstrated that socialism and its principles are a viable political programme and that the electorate will support those who declare their faith and stick to their principles just as much as they are likely to support those who betray their principles and preach compromise as a basis for achieving their own personal ambitions.

CHAPTER TWENTY NINE

1984 Miners' Strike

Just weeks after the Tony Benn by-election the area was thrown into twelve months of bitter struggle in what was to become a landmark in the industrial and political history of the British labour movement. The miners strike was significant in so much as their principal stand was on the humanitarian and moral issue of defending pit closures for jobs and the future life of the mining community, and not for money.

The background of solidarity and unity of the miners, based on their long history and traditions particularly connected with 1926 and onwards, had always influenced the action of the miners and the way the rest of the movement regarded them. But in the late 70s and early 80s there had already been redundancy, early retirement and pit closures so that, in the main, those who were influenced by the traditions of 1926 and the struggles of the early mining communities were no longer in the industry. And there was a feeling when the strike started that there might be difficulties because of the fact that the people who could remember the early battles were no longer there, that this was a younger generation who had been brought up outside of the period's conditions. But this was one of the most positive things to come out of the strike. The young men were being involved possibly for the first time in industrial and political battles and they responded magnificently. At a local level there developed a new set of leaders, a new group of committed activists who were fearless and responsible in defence of their class and the emergence of these new young activists is a plus for the movement.

One other good thing to come out of the strike was the development of the women's support groups. In previous battles and disputes in the mining industry the miners wives had always played a part but never before did they play such an important role in the context of the strike and in mobilising support for the issues involved as the women's support groups did in this dispute. International support was also far more widespread than before where local women went to America, while organisations in France, Holland and many other places regularly collected for the support groups. Many got their first glimpse of international socialism and some have tried to maintain these links, which is a very good and positive fact to come out of the struggle.

There has been much discussion on the strike itself, on its leadership and its direction and the effect of its defeat on the movement. Never in the history of the establishment and government has any government prepared so thoroughly and been prepared to spend so much money on winning an industrial dispute. They recognised the importance of the strike on the country's political and industrial future development and they spent many millions and millions of pounds on mobilising everything and everybody to make sure the miners were defeated. The tragedy was that the labour movement did not mobilise at all and repeated the error of allowing the miners to fight alone. True, there was magnificent financial support from various sections of the movement. But it fell far short of what the miners needed to win. There was a lot of twaddle talked about the necessity of holding a ballot which were really only excuses used by those who wanted to undermine the strength of the miners rather than wishing them well in victory. The union was right to proceed by taking its decisions by its own democratic processes. In my time in industry it was a common-place principle which I always used that if you were discussing whether or not somebody should maintain a job, or there was a question of redundancy and you were fighting against it, the first principle which you have to observe is to never allow a list to appear of those who are going to be made redudant before you have had a ballot on action. Because it is too easy when somebody knows that they are not involved to then decide through a ballot that they do not want to do anything about somebody else losing their job.

I still think, though, we should learn by our experiences. If the TUC and national leadership failed to give support then much more should have been done at grass roots level. Picketing and mass rallies alone will not win industrial battles. I feel much more effort should have been placed in both mobilising and involving the miners themselves so that they understood what was happening in the dispute. Local conferences organised through trades councils could have built up support both locally and nationally to influence support in the TUC, the Labour party and other national trade union organisations. The role played by the leadership of the Labour party and the TUC was a scandal and the perfect example of where reformism in the movement can lead. Everyone was standing back because they were afraid and Kinnock was being pasted up on whether or not he supported violence so that he was dithering about like a jelly in a pot. When it was obvious that no decision was going to go through the National Executive Committee, the movement should have developed at grass roots the demand for action and forced the Executive to shift.

There was not enough clear recognition on behalf of the rest of the movement that their own future was involved in the struggle, not merely that of the miners. It is my firm personal opinion that the miners could have won. All it wanted was the extra push from the rest of the movement which would not have cost a great deal. The miners fought bravely and with determination but once again they were let down by the rest of the movement and their defeat will leave a scar that will be with the movement for the rest of its days.

CHAPTER THIRTY

Developing and Establishing Britain's Largest May Day Celebrations

Trade unions should not merely respond to issues but they should lead and put forward programmed policies where they can achieve and develop the ideas of trade unionism itself. While the union has to deal with the economic problems of its members, at the same time it must lead them into something a bit wider and broader.

This is what we tried to do on the shop floor at Sheepbridge. We had battles about piece work prices every day of our lives but we used to try to impress upon the people that if they wanted a good shop floor organisation that was confident, efficient and capable of dealing with the piece price they also had to have one that mobilised the support on a wider basis which could go outside the plant because of its prestige. Sometimes I tend to think that the movement, particularly in the factories, has become too reliant on what they think has been written down either by legislation or agreements rather than realising it is important for a shop floor organisation to have a voice which will be accepted by management.

For instance, one of the biggest problems at Sheepbridge and in other places is the question of overtime. So we developed a policy whereby nobody was allowed to work overtime unless it was endorsed by the shop stewards committee or the section shop stewards so we had control over the matter. In this way the management could not waltz out on to the shop floor and demand people work overtime on certain days because it was the decision of the stewards that they — and only they — could give that permission. There was no question of us utilising the situation to be awkward or antagonistic, just that we were able to be in charge and take other matters into consideration. Legislation and education is fine but they have never, ever got to be looked upon as a substitute for trade union organisation.

During the '50s my own union made me president of its divisional committee which subsequently elected me onto the national committee in 1956 when Bill Carron, or Lord Carron, held sway in the balance of forces, which within the union were on a knife's edge. It was a very interesting and important period because the split between Left and Right was so finely balanced that on most occasions there was only one vote in it. It is worth remembering that during this time, including the period when Hugh Scanlon took over, the Left in the AEU played a very important role in developing the working class movement inspite of the fact that it never had a Left voting majority. This was done mainly by winning allies and getting the support of various groups of people and not, as many presumed, by the Left having a built in majority. However the right-wing came up with the idea of postal ballots for members to elect their leaders rather than voting through their branches, and it was the biggest mistake the Left made in allowing them to do it.

The introduction of the postal vote certainly allowed the right-wing to become entrenched within the AEU. At branches at least those who turned up were sufficiently motivated to vote. They may have been influenced by the active members but they were usually people who knew what the issues and arguments were. With the postal vote you pass over this influence to the media, who are usually only concerned with whether the candidates are Reds or support Reds. The question of whether they fight for better wages, improved conditions, improved safety regulations, greater democracy in the union in the sense of greater freedom for those on the shop floor is never mentioned. All the press concentrates on is that someone is a Red and consequently should not get the vote.

As a result now in the AEU and any other union that conducts this policy we have the biggest collection of nonentities that has ever been seen in the British trade union movement. This not only stagnates the organisation but takes away all credibility from those who supposedly exercise the power.

In Chesterfield the Trades Council virtually went out of existence in the aftermath of the '26 general strike. It was resurrected in 1937 or '38 with the help of Bob Tate, a member of the shopworkers union USDAW, who became its secretary. When he was called up for war service Reg Brightmore took over until after the war, followed by a succession of various people. With the development of the cold war and the anti-Soviet campaign following Churchill's speech about the Iron Curtain, the Trades Union Congress re-instituted the black circular which meant that no Communist party member could be a delegate to a Trades Council. Not all Trades Councils applied the rule but Chesterfield did so that when I moved to the town in 1953 we decided to start a campaign to gradually win confidence and acceptance and get the decision rescinded.

This was eventually done and I went on to the Trades Council as a delegate determined to try and develop it into a campaigning organisation that could be felt as being useful to and part of the general trade union movement. After a while we were able to change the Trades Council from a sort of once-a-month social gathering of delegates to a campaigning organisation playing a role in the labour movement. In 1960 I was elected President and remained in that position for fifteen years until, at the age of seventy, I decided it was time to step down. In that time we strove hard to maintain May Day and fought hard to establish a march. Then it was generally held on the first Sunday in May but we managed to get it moved to the first Saturday in May and introduced meetings so at least we could march through the town and catch the market shoppers and establish some sort of recognition of the trade union movement in the area.

We also organised celebrations to mark the centenary of the TUC in 1968 when we not only ran trips to the national celebrations but took over the Civic Theatre and put on D.H. Lawrence's Daughter-in-law play because of its mining and working class interest. For one whole evening we occupied the theatre issued special invitations to all the various people connected with the trade union and labour movement, had a special commemoration programme drawn up and then afterwards put on a buffet in the theatre's foyer. It was a great success and gave the Trades Council a good deal of publicity.

Then in 1977 the Labour government passed legislation declaring that the first Monday in May would be a statutory workers holiday. It was, of course, a typical social democrat compromise, dodging the issue of making the statutory holiday actually on the first day of May and responding to the plea from employers organisations that the holiday should be on the first Monday of the month. Nevertheless, the Trades Council immediately recognised its importance and decided to call meetings to try and establish it as a day of workers demonstration and celebration. The employers also immediately moved to try to get the holiday transferred and tagged onto other holidays throughout the year, claiming it would avoid a separate shut down, and in some cases conned the workers along the way.

Myself and Beryl centre taken in the main marquee at the first Chesterfield May Day Gala in 1978.

We tried to impress on all factory and office workers the necessity of fighting for the bank holiday to be taken on the first Monday in May so we could celebrate May Day. The Trades Council organised joint meetings of the workers representatives in the various factories and organisations to try to get this understanding across and to get their help in establishing May Day as a day for the labour movement, which we coined the People's May Day. There were many arguments with shop stewards and all sorts of people

'Bas just shouted "Mayday, Mayday"!—then he sank just here'

(With thanks to Mac of the Daily Mail)

May Day cartoon — taken from one of the earlier gala programmes.

about us establishing this as an independent day to march and demonstrate, mainly based on the fact that previously we had not been able to muster tremendous crowds to take part in our marches. Some argued it would be better to try to co-operate with Sheffield or other towns in a joint march rather than establish our own May Day. But I was convinced that we should go ahead because if we could pull it off it would put the Trades Council on the map. It is ironic that the May Day demonstration in Chesterfield is now the largest and most successful in the country, while Sheffield does not even hold one.

Our whole approach was a People's May Day, not merely a meeting but a free family day out with political education and political activity. It took, and still takes, 12 months of planning and costs thousands of pounds each year to stage but the money is raised through the movement and by and large we cover the cost. This is mainly due to the tremendous help and encouragement of the North Derbyshire NUM who, once we had convinced them of the viability of the idea, agreed to virtually underwrite the cost and give us their unstinting support.

Now we hold the largest event of its kind with more people participating and attending than in large centres such as London, Glasgow or Birmingham. While May Day activities seem to have been declining throughout the rest of the country, in Chesterfield they have heightened the whole of the political activity throughout the movement, giving every section a boost and focus to work for. And so what started out as a very tentative idea has proved a tremendous success so that now we can proudly say it leads the country and is the basis on which the Chesterfield and North Derbyshire Trades Council activities and prestige rests.

The People's March for Jobs in 1981 enabled the Trades Council to build up support for the unemployed across a wide section of society involving the labour movement, local councils, the churches — and in some cases even the bishops — and social organisations. I suppose you could say the movement had advanced since the hunger marches of the '30s, organised by the National Unemployed Workers Movement, in so much as the March for Jobs was at least officially sponsored by the TUC. It was a big jump from the days when delegations of unemployed workers actually had to literally break into the TUC conference and raise the question of their plight from the public galleries, only to be physically ejected for daring to direct the attention of the Congress to the issue. Indeed the response we received and the reception given to the marchers made Chesterfield one of the successes of the march.

But while the People's March for Jobs was successful in raising the issues of the unemployed it also raised some questions for the movement. Why is it, for example, that a government which creates four million unemployed is tolerated by society? No one would have believed that a government which creates unemployment at today's level would be able to continue to exist and rule. It is true that unemployment does not create the scarring poverty of the '30s but the indignities, loss of pride, the destruction of purpose of living is just the same. And it exists with barely a ripple on the political millpond. There does not seem to be any communication between the movement on the one hand and the unemployed on the other. Nowadays the government has managed to keep the unemployed at a distance whereas in the 1930s daily meetings were conducted outside the labour exchanges and there was much agitation, with large numbers of hunger marches being just part of that agitation.

Week in and week out the unemployed were active in their organisations in bringing to the notice of the rest of the population the obscenity of the people living in riches and luxury against the plight of the unemployed. Surely the labour movement can find a way of arousing the sullen anger of these people that could develop a movement which could give new hope to them, and at the same time to the movement itself. I believe one of the answers must be for the development of a new National Unemployed Workers movement, sponsored and affiliated to the TUC, whose job would be to deal with the problems of the unemployed, dealing with the necessary case work but, more importantly, organising and being a voice of the unemployed and expressing their demands and aspirations to the authorities in every sphere. I am sure the whole movement would benefit from such a development.

CHAPTER THIRTY ONE

Training and Young People

With the development in further education that was introduced after the war, particularly in the engineering industry where there was union interest in the standard of improvement in apprentices' education, it was decided to play a more active role on the board of governors of the Chesterfield College of Technology. The union had always had a representative on the board but it has usually gone to whoever was prepared to take it. But with these new developments it was agreed to try to take a more serious interest in the matter and we agreed that the union officials should become the union's representatives on the board, and so I was appointed to the college in 1964.

I found the experience not only extremely worthwhile but quite humbling. I remember that while there were all sorts of criticisms being flung around about the irresponsibility of youth, the students showed they were the complete opposite to the image the general public had of youngsters. Every week thousands would attend the great variety of courses, and as I met and spoke with them I found that their reasons for being there were for their own professional development and that most were very capable young men and women. I then formed the opinion that all those who criticised youngsters as a group of irresponsible people with no knowledge of the world should have been made to have taken a compulsory course of training themselves. Because after moving with the youngsters and seeing how they operated I am certain that they knew much more about the world than ever our generation did at their age.

Because the local authorities fund the colleges the board of governors was dominated by a virtual majority of people representing the county council and local authorities representing the particular political colour of whatever party dominated the county council at that time. Therefore, with the swing of the political pendulum that affected the county council the membership of the college's governors was never very stable. As a direct nominee of my trade union I was fortunate not to be affected by the constant change and remained a member of the board for twenty years. Being controlled by the county council always meant trying to provide the best possible education under budget constraints yet, whatever the colour of the government, we always seemed to be involved in the same arguments. Whether it was a Tory or a Labour regime, despite the need to invest in education, each ruling group would be trying to justify the necessity of the cuts and restrictions that they were imposing. It always seemed to me to be particularly obscene for people of whatever hue to raise these arguments in one of the richest countries of the world which had plenty of money but where the priority of spending was determined by other factors.

In the 1970s Labour had control of the county council and I was nominated by the Labour representatives on the board to chair the governors. It was a position I held for six years and during that time it is fair to say that I managed to exert my influence by insisting that my point of view should be considered. My aim was that the college should be seen as a progressive provision of facilities for the youngsters, and while Chairman I got into the habit of regularly going into the students common room to chat to them and their union representatives about any problems they had with courses or classes. It certainly had not been done before, and I am not sure if it has ever been done since, but it proved to be a very valuable exercise. I did not agree with all their problems and would sometimes tell them straight that I thought they were talking a load of baloney. But on other occasions I would listen to the grievances and try to sort out something. For instance, once they complained bitterly about the length of time they had to wait in the canteen to get their lunch. After discussing the matter with them I then went and stood in the queue and timed it. It turned out that really it was no worse than the situation in most works canteens or other places, but I was able to get the youngsters and the canteen people to discuss the matter and sort out the problem.

A student's union in a college like Chesterfield rarely succeeds in getting off the ground. It has nothing to do with the quality of the youngsters but with the fact that most of the students are there part-time with a job to go to, and really a union needs to be run by full-time students who usually do not start taking an interest until they have been there for at least a year. So with constant change it is difficult for anyone to put in any motivation or a stamp of authority on it. My biggest disappointment came with the change in political colour at the county council when all the Labour representatives were ousted from the board and replaced by Tories. When it came to the election of Chairman the Tories obviously nominated against me and I lost it solely on the basis of the votes of the two student representatives. I am convinced they did not know what they were doing but that they had been influenced by some of the staff who did know what they were doing. And I felt it significant that of the people who I had worked with as Chairman — who included direct representatives from industry — I managed to win support, but that the two who tipped the scales were students attending their first meeting and who were unaware of the set up, yet were so enthusiastic to put up their hand to make sure that a new Tory Chairman was installed.

One of the good things which I experienced through the college and took part in was the Training Board for Industry. These were set up by the government to provide proper training with proper monitoring for the youngsters in the various engineering, construction and other industries. While these were not by any means perfect the fact they provided an increased basis of training with monitoring and examinations and certificates at the end of it all was a distinct advance on anything we had ever had before. Unfortunately the Tory government preferred to spend its time demolishing them and set up in their place the so-called Youth Opportunity Schemes and, later, Youth Training Schemes, Community Programmes, Employment Training and a mass array of similar projects.

In my view these new schemes are aimed at reducing the numbers on the unemployment register and providing cheap labour for industry. Previously anyone on a training course was never considered as being employed and was therefore always included among the unemployment figures. Any government really serious about training would have used the training boards and the technical colleges to provide schemes with an adequate wage for all those taking part in them. I am sure that with the resources that are obviously available and the dedication of a lot of people involved in this type of work, it would have been possible to have provided a full training scheme within the normal education system for all youngsters who left school.

At the inception of the Youth Schemes the government set up regional boards to administer them which included trade union representatives, and I was appointed to one of these seats on the East Midlands regional board. Initially it was fairly slow to get off the ground because most people could not understand what could or could not be done. But as soon as a lot of the smart Alecs in industry and elsewhere saw what was possible then ideas for schemes came flooding in. Our job was to endorse the provision of people to work on the various schemes and projects. No doubt some of them provided for social benefit but not many contained any real training. I was always in the dilemma of recognising schemes which were of no benefit to anyone except those putting forward the project, and knowing that if it was thrown out the youngsters who would have been employed on the scheme would remain on the dole. Should I condemn them to further long periods of being on the dole or provide them with a half-baked chance of getting some work?

The schemes operated so that the youngsters were paid by the government's Manpower Services Commission while the organisations putting forward the project provided the materials. So we used to have a flood of applications from all sorts of groups, particularly charitable and social organisations. At one time there were so many applications for cleaning up church yards in nearly every vicinity that I was moved to comment that we appeared to be doing more for the dead than we were for the living. And as the scheme progressed I became more disenchanted with it so that when the time came to re-appoint the representatives I decided to let the union make a fresh nomination. But I believe that while ever the schemes exist and the TUC insists it wants to be part and parcel of them then it is necessary for robust trade union representatives to play their part. For while there are many reservations it is a fact that without some careful vetting and monitoring by the trade union movement the schemes would be a thousand times worse. But I am convinced that if they only utilised the expertise and knowledge available within colleges of further education instead of preferring to rely on all sorts of agencies, the project would be of far more value.

When the college merged with the Art College I decided it was time to step aside and allow new people to become involved in its new future right from the start. At the last meeting of the old board of governors in July 1984 I was given a citation from the governors, staff and students for my work with the college, which pleased me very much and made me realise that the town does not seem to appreciate its college, which runs all sorts of courses and classes and which has gained a large number of awards, or realise what a wonderful organisation it is. The ultimate idea is for the re-organisation of education and a tertiary college in Chesterfield when maybe the public will become more interested in what the college is doing and what it can provide for the community.

CHAPTER THIRTY TWO

The National Health Service

During my early days as a Trades Council delegate I recall we were regularly asked for nominations to the Hospital Management committee, and although we returned the nomination forms the general feeling was that no one would ever be accepted as these jobs and positions were kept for tame middle-class do-gooders. In the main this was true in both theory and practice so when I filled in my form I considered it very unlikely that I would be involved in any further activities. Then, out of the blue, came a letter of appointment to the Chesterfield Hospital Management committee inviting me to go and see the administrator at his Scarsdale Hospital offices to discuss the matter. The committee served all the major hospitals in the area and members were split up into sub-committees, visiting committees and other committees dealing with various branches of hospital activity. I found the whole experience very interesting and enjoyable in the sense it enabled me to get around and see what was happening in the various hospitals. But whatever else was affecting the health service it was certainly not democracy.

The hospital management committee represented various interests of the voluntary organisations, those who work for the hospitals, hospital Friends, local authorities and so on. But certainly the most powerful interests were the medical ones. The consultants and general practitioners had their own committee which evolved as the most authoritive when it came to the question of spending money. I soon came up against the term "clinical judgement" which, during my course of activity with the health service, I got to both love and hate. In all sorts of situations if the medical fraternity claimed that whatever had been done was a matter of "clinical judgement" then they could not be challenged by any of the lay members because it was felt they could not make a decision. Only the trained professional, it was claimed, could take "clinical judgement" decisions. It was a very difficult problem to try to get around because if you argued someone ought to have been treated differently then you were quickly reminded that it was a question of "clinical judgement" and you could not make any comment in that sphere.

The National Health Service was set up to provide treatment and medical care at the point of need for all without payment. And it is said that when Nye Bevan was asked how he got the consultants to agree to join in the NHS he replied: "I stuffed their mouths with gold". The closer you got to the health service and the more intimately you got to know its problems the more your appreciated the truth of that statement. It is my opinion that while ever we allow private practice in the NHS we shall always be plagued with vested interest working for its own ends. The only solution is a complete salaried service with everybody having to participate. The re-organisation of the health service in 1974 was perhaps an improvement in that it set up the Area Health Authorities covering a wider area, but again with the missing ingredients of democratic representation and accountability. The NHS was a wonderful idea and despite all its problems and weaknesses does a remarkable job for the community. But unfortunately because of its lack of democratic accountability it has been hijacked by vested interests. The various professional organisations of people employed in the health service such as consultants, GPs, dentists, opticians, have all believed the NHS was a milk cow which existed to serve their own special interests and have resisted any efforts towards democratic control.

So when the Area Health Authorities were set up the government also established the Community Health Councils to give the public some say in the running of the health service, and I was appointed by the regional health authority to serve on the North Derbyshire Community Health Council. Its conception as a public watchdog was fine even if idealistic, but it has failed because it does not have any powerful teeth. It is a completely advisory body and although it is important to voice your opinion you never have the power to change whatever the establishment team has decided. To play a vital part in the NHS the council needs separate funding and a membership chosen on a more democratic basis, with more independence and responsibility. For two years I was its Chairman when I considered it was important to keep a different point of view to the fore other than the establishment one. In some instances it was possible to build allies and get agreement for reconsideration of some issues, but in most cases it was not.

I suppose that by taking an interest in the health service I was following my father who had been a miners' representative on the hospital committee in the '30s. Just recently Chesterfield has opened a new district hospital and I recall that my father was part of the delegation from the committee who went and bought land at Ashgate on which to build the new hospital. The ambulance station was put in position at the corner of Ashgate to eventually serve the new hospital, and a house was built for the future new hospital secretary. But when we came to discuss detailed plans the regional planners suggested the new hospital would be in the wrong place at Ashgate because it was on the periphery of the area, and they wanted it somewhere more central and accessible to the M1 motorway. So we arranged to swop the land with the local authority for some land it owned at Calow which had been earmarked for a heliport. Some argued that Scarsdale hospital and the health and chest clinic should have been demolished and the whole of the land used for the new hospital. I suppose the decision as to whether it is in the right place or not depends very much on where you live. But it is interesting to note that while the original plans were drawn up in the '30s it took another fifty years before they came to fruition.

During the course of my work with the health service I developed a curious relationship with Fred Short. Fred and his family had been connected with the hospital management in Chesterfield for a great number of years. He was managing director of Pearsons pottery and his step-father, Theo Pearson, had also been a Chairman of the Hospital Management committee. Fred would agree that he was regarded as a ruthless private industry owner and used to joke over his relationship with the trade unions on his own plant. But his loyalty and dedication to making the hospital service as good as it possibly could be was undeniable. In every other sphere and every other attitude we were at daggers drawn and bitterly opposed to each other. Yet on the hospital management committee we were able to work together for the same aims. And I remember asking him once why he thought this was so and he replied: "I know you have come onto this Hospital Management committee because of your principles and what you are fighting for. You are neither filling in time nor being a do-gooder and therefore I respect your integrity as you respect mine". And so we fought many joint battles.

When he later retired as Chairman of the local Disablement committee they decided to present him with a couple of silver candlesticks and I was asked to make the presentation. I thought it a peculiar choice because obviously there were no two people who had more differing views about the problems of the world and life in general than Fred Short and myself. But the committee said that we seemed to get on well together in meetings and they would like me to do it. So I made the presentation and told him that I had agreed to do so on the understanding that when he had the candlesticks on his table he had only to use red candles in them, and if he put anything other than red in them they would certainly not succeed to burn properly.

At a later stage when we were opening a new ward at Walton Hospital which was being named after Fred Short he was invited to unveil the plaque. Speaking afterwards he said he had been present at a number of similar events honouring his work for the hospital and health service, and he turned to the audience and said that he had previously been presented with some silver candlesticks which were now in position in his new house and his new dining room and he wanted to assure everybody present that there were only red candlesticks being used in them. Quite a number of people who were not involved in the first presentation were mystified as to what this was all about as it was mentioned specifically for my benefit, but it highlights the curious relationship which developed between us.

At the moment the NHS is going through a bad patch and if the Tories maintain their aim they will destroy it. While the health service is probably the country's biggest employer and a major national organisation it operates on scandalously low wages and, in many cases, in archaic conditions. The love, care and dedication of the staff at all levels is undeniable and to envisage life without the health service would be disastrous. Yet society still exploits the dedication of people who work in it and mealie mouthed hypocrites keep declaring that while we can afford guns and bombs we cannot afford to pay our people to take care of the sick and old.

CHAPTER THIRTY THREE

Socialist Travels

Because of my work in the movement it was a natural development for me to become interested in the progress of the Socialist countries in Eastern Europe. I had already witnessed the development in its infancy of the Soviet Union during my visit there in 1935 so that when thirty years later a friend of mine in London asked if I would like to go on a trip to Czechoslovakia, I was very keen to make the journey. The trip was organised by Progressive Tours, set up particularly to organise holidays in the Socialist countries and arranged mainly, in those days, through the trade unions for people of the labour movement. I remember it cost £37 a head for a fifteen-day holiday, but even at those prices we had to look long and hard at our resources before Beryl and I decided to go on our very first holiday.

We travelled to Harwich where we caught a ferry to Ostend from where we went by train to Prague. And what a journey that was. There was no sleeping accommodation so you just had to nod off where you were sitting and it took an eternity to get there. I was convinced then that there had to be better ways of travelling across Europe than by train. When we eventually arrived in Prague we were met by the trade union and a representative from the travel agency who put us on a coach to take us to our hotel. As, in the case of most big city areas around railway stations or airports, everywhere looked most dreary and dilapidated by the time we got to the hotel we decided we had had enough and just went to bed feeling exhausted and very disappointed.

But the next morning when we got up rested and refreshed and the sun was shining we found Prague to be a different world. It is one of the most beautiful cities in the world with marvellous buildings in their mediaeval settings and a river sprung with remarkable noble bridges. Altogether we spent a week there looking at all the main buildings and facilities, and visiting factories where we received the most wonderful hospitality.

Then from Prague we went to one of the spa towns called Marianske Lazne which, in its pre-war days, had been the famous spa where the rich went to take the cure, including the Prince of Wales Edward the Seventh, who apparently used to take his girlfriends with him. So they built him a special bath and when we were invited to try it out we felt the wheel had turned full circle, and I can always claim to have used the same bath as the Prince of Wales. It was a wonderful holiday because we made great friends with other international delegations from all parts of the world, particularly the socialist countries.

When I got back home I was invited to report on my experiences to the shop stewards committee and afterwards a number of them raised the possibility of us being able to sponsor a group from the area, primarily based on our own factory but involving other factories and organisations. So we contacted Progressive Tours who agreed that it we could recruit somewhere up to nearly thirty people they would make the necessary arrangements.

So the following year we again organised a holiday in Czechoslovakia but on this occasion took the train from Sheffield to Harwich, crossed over by ferry to Ostend and then picked up a Dutch coach and driver to take us the rest of the way and to stay with us throughout the holiday. He was a wonderful driver who seemed to know Europe's back streets like the back of his hand. Our plan was to make our way to the Czech border then go to Pilsen where they make the famous beer — and where the large Skoda plant is. But when we got to the Czech border something was wrong and they would not let us through. As I had organised the trip I was delegated the responsibility of trying to sort it out, and was allowed across to the check point. But I could not speak Czech and they could not speak English so we were at stalemate. There was the coach full of people on the other side while I was trying to understand why we were not allowed to travel on. I was sitting on the steps of the customs office trying to think of how to solve this problem when a man and a woman drew up in a car and the lady got out to clear her visa speaking in Czech. Then the man, who turned out to be her husband, spoke in English and in a dialect that indicated he was obviously a native.

So I immediately approached him and discovered that his wife was a Czech who he had married during the war. I explained our difficulty and the fact that I could not find out why we could not continue on our journey and she translated for me. It turned out that because of a Post Office strike in Britain the necessary visas and papers for the driver had not arrived at the Dutch coach office and so the driver was without proper credentials, which were probably somewhere between Britain and Holland. By this time a representative from the trade union who had come to meet us at the border had arrived and although he could not speak English we managed, through the help of this woman, to influence the officials sufficiently to allow us to go on to Pilsen where we would have to raise the matter with the authorities and get a supplementary set of papers for the driver to take us any further.

Eventually we set off again and after all we had been through we felt so relieved to finally be on our way that we began, as the British usually do, to sing. Later the trade union representative told me he was astonished that after all our upset we seemed perfectly happy and were singing and that it has given him an insight into the British character. For he claimed that had it been a coachload of Czech people or anybody on the continent then by that time they would have been pulling the bus to pieces instead of merely accepting the fact that these mishaps do occur and to be cheerful about it.

But I was fuming that our interpreter had not been at the border to meet us and was told she would be waiting for us at our hotel in Pilsen. But when we arrived it was left to me to try and sort out the rooms for everybody, so by this time I was getting a bit browned off and demanded that this elusive interpreter be found, at which point she suddenly appeared. Eve turned out to have a marvellous knowledge of the English language and I gamble if anyone met her today they would not know she is a Czech. She was one of the best couriers we have ever had and she still comes to visit us whenever she is in England on a job.

Our first visit was to a castle. Now some thought to themselves: 'All this way across Europe just to see a castle". But it was a very special kind of castle, owned by the Skoda family and taken over as a trade union holiday centre. It stood in its own terrific grounds with lakes and every other sporting facility you could imagine. So we went and enjoyed ourselves and met other trade unionists having a holiday there. The following day was one of the highlights for some as we visited the famous Pilsen brewery. After being shown around we were taken into the board room and invited to drink as much beer as we liked. We had arranged to go on to Lidice in the afternoon but as a result of the Pilsen beer we had to postpone our plans until the next day.

Lidice was a Czech mining village but when the Gauleiter of Czechoslovakia was assassinated in Prague the Germans said a letter they had intercepted indicated that some of those responsible had come from Lidice. As a matter of revenge, therefore, the troops went in, collected all the males over fifteen years of age and shot them. The women and younger children were herded together and sent to concentration camps and the whole village was then bulldozed so, said Hitler, to wipe it from the face of the earth. During the war the British miners decided to launch a campaign so Lidice could live again and become the symbol of the rejection of fascism. So after the war the village was rebuilt and all the trade union branches in Britain were asked to contribute to a memorial rose garden and buy a rose. They were sent from Wheatcroft nurseries in Nottingham where Harry Wheatcroft, who was head of the nursery and sympathetic to the labour and trade union movement, chose the roses and made arrangements for them to be taken over and planted. Now anybody who goes to Lidice can see the British rose garden in the new resurrected village as a symbol of the victory over fascism. There is a museum and a film which they managed to get out of the German archives of the destruction of the village and the lady in charge of it all used to live in the village as a girl and managed to survive the concentration camps.

Based on the fact we now had some experience in organising holidays we decided to look further afield and chose East Germany. Most people, even those in the movement, had a mental picture of a dull grey country with people dressed in drab clothes, mainly based on what they had read in the press. When you actually get there the very opposite is the truth. I would think that of all the countries which developed and advanced from the destruction of the war the one which has made the greatest strides is East Germany. People are bright and cheerful while the standard of living is possibly the best in East Europe and a complete contradiction of the picture portrayed in the West.

Our first visit was spent in a trade union holiday centre in Sernrode which is in the Hartz mountains and near some of the old mediaeval towns. We had marvellous weather and were able to walk in the woods, having evening sing-songs and many other very enjoyable experiences. And I recall that after being there for a week we were sitting on the balcony outside our room when one of our group shouted to me and asked. "Is it true that we are behind the Iron Curtain?". So, a bit astonished, I said: "Of course we are". And he said: "Well just explain it will you to the wife because she won't believe me". And because his wife was thoroughly enjoying herself and having the time of her life she would not believe we were behind the Iron Curtain, and later admitted that had she realised we were going behind the Iron Curtain she probably would have refused to have come.

In the pre-war days in Sheffield we had a group of Czech refugees who came from Sudetenland after Hitler moved in before taking over the whole of Czechoslovakia. We built up strong friendships with these political refugees, the leader of whom was a man called Robert Zapf who stayed in Sheffield until after the war. When he returned he went to Weimar and over the years continued to keep in touch by exchanging Christmas cards. So while in East Germany we decided we would try to go to Weimar and see if we could find Robert. By now he would be getting on for eighty but we easily found his home and renewed our acquaintance. He was so pleased to see us and sent out for some special German cakes, while we had brought him a very large bottle of coffee as a present because it was very difficult and expensive to get over there in those days. We were very pleased to have had the opportunity of seeing Robert again because he died a couple of years later, although we still hear from his daughter every Christmas.

Some years later a small group of us went to Poland and in fact I visited the country twice, once to Warsaw and the second time to Zakopane, which is a beautiful resort with small wooden hotels and which served some of the best food I have ever tasted anywhere. But one of the things which always worried me — and I think my worries have since born fruit — was the strength and overall pervading attitudes of the Catholic church there.

I remember in Warsaw being taken to see this massive Cathedral which they proudly announced was provided by the State. They had done a marvellous job of re-building the city and of even trying to reproduce some of the mediaeval buildings in the old market square. This Cathedral was brick built with people inside doing their devout curtseying and crossing and I recall one of our party asking me what I thought to it all. My reply was a bit like the Duke of Wellington's: "I didn't know whether it frightened them but by God it frightened me". In so many cases the one thing that is holding back progress is the Catholic church and while ever it is there and allowed to exist and has the power, authority and influence over the people, as it does in Poland, then there will always be difficulties because the Catholic church does not want to allow any authority other than its own. In every sphere and in every situation it has been on the side of reaction so that if they allow progress then they must allow for the fact that there has to be other thinking with people allowed to embrace other theories and other practices other than the church.

126

Poland is the strongest Catholic country in the world with more Catholic population than anywhere else which is very deeply rooted so the church becomes the busiest place in town. They preach, like any other religion, that there is no need to do anything about the conditions on earth because all you have to do is make sure you are good enough to enjoy the next world. So the Polish Communist party has got the terrific job of trying to develop a progressive solution to the country's problems while at the same time carrying along this heavy burden of the Catholic church. I believe they have got the greatest task of any Communist party in the world, particularly in Eastern Europe.

One of the best holidays that we ever had was in Hungary where we spent a week in Budapest and a week at Lake Balaton. Budapest is a marvellous city on the Danube and we were met by Hungarian trade union representatives who produced a programme of visits including a circus, a gypsy orchestra, travelling up the Danube and eating at a well known restaurant. It was all astonishing value for money, with the highlight being a trip on the river boat where we had wine and cream cakes. At the end a coach was waiting to take us to a castle on a hill, but by the time we had drunk all this Hungarian wine and eaten all the Hungarian food there were not many of us who could walk straight to that castle.

Lake Balaton is the largest inland lake in Europe but you cannot imagine its size because it disappears over the horizon. Those who wanted to bathe in the marvellously warm water could walk out for half-a-mile or more and still find the water only came up to their chest. In our hotel was another group of holiday makers who turned out to be Vietnamese soldiers who had been pulled out of the front line of the war and sent to Hungary for a break. Although we couldn't speak their language and they couldn't speak ours we had great fun trying to translate. They were very friendly and in the evening we would try to teach them some of our songs. When it came to saying our farewells we bought some drink and everyone went round giving little badges and presents. One of the women on the trip always refers to the fact that meeting the Vietnamese was one of the greatest experiences of her life time.

Our trip to the Soviet Union in 1975 was given to us as a perk for the number of years we had spent in the movement, and there is no doubt it was a marvellous holiday. It is a place which if anybody wants to talk about or understand it should really be visited. An awful lot of rubbish about the country is put out by the media which, on visiting, is so obviously and patently not true. People there are human, normal people like anywhere else in the world. They are jolly people who love a bit of fun and who have a similar sense of humour to ourselves when it comes to telling jokes about their leaders.

For instance I remember being at a banquet when someone who worked at the Kremlin was telling a joke which, when translated, turned out to be about the establishment. This man applied to join the Party and had to appear before the committee to be vetted. He was asked if he understood the seriousness of the step he was about to take and he said, yes. Did he understand that from now on that, if accepted, he would have to be an example for his fellow men and women, work the hardest, be the best worker and never be late for work, and he said he understood. Did he understand that he would have to study and become proficient in Marxism and Leninism, and he said, yes. And did he understand that wine, women and song could no longer be enjoyed because his approach to life would have to be serious, and he said, yes. Finally he was asked if he understood that at some time it may be necessary to give his life for the Party. And he said: "Oh yes, I understand that for who wants a bloody life like that".

When people judge the Soviet Union they should ask themselves are the vast majority of people better off day in and day out, week in and week out, year in and year out than they were before, and if the answer is yes then you can afford the fact of an indiscretion here and a diversion there. Often the people who are belly-aching about leaving the country are those who have been given the best the Soviet Union can give them, such as leading ballet dancers and writers, who have had the best university education but who, for some reason, are conned into believing that the grass is greener on the other side. But I gamble that there is no one ordinary person in the Soviet Union who wants to leave.

That does not mean to say that there are no mistakes. Undoubtedly mistakes have been made but they have got to be measured always by the common yardstick of how do the millions of ordinary people fare. If it is better now than last year and it appears that they will be better off next year than this year then I think that should be the judge. The only reason why we get bogged down in the problem of human rights is because there is bound to be somebody somewhere who will probably get the bad end of the stick and hurt in the system, but we cannot afford to destroy it just for that. For despite all its difficulties and problems they have by and large remained true to our socialist theories and it is still the best expression of them that we have. Certainly it is my greatest wish to return and see it again before I finish my work in the movement.

CHAPTER THIRTY FOUR

Retirement and Freedom

When you are working among a large number of people it is difficult to define whether you have any personal impact, and I suppose that during my years at Sheepbridge I had organised hundreds of retirement presentations. So when my own time came I was told by the lads on the shop stewards committee in no uncertain terms that this was one event which I would not be allowed to have anything to do with on the organisational side.

When the management learned I was due to retire that September in 1975 they asked me if I actually intended to do so because they felt I had been so involved that I would not want to make such a drastic change to my life. They also asked if I was all right for money and of course I said no, like everybody else who has only got the state pension to rely on. Because in spite of nearly forty years service with Sheepbridge there was no pension for me to enjoy. So they suggested that I might like to stay on in an advisory capacity and visit the works one or two days a week to offer advice to the shop stewards on the one hand and the management on the other. Of course I refused because the situation would have merely led to me being the sole arbiter with nobody prepared to solve anything. The management would have suggested it be left until the oracle came and the shop stewards committee would have done the same. So I decided that it would be in the best interest of the movement to make a clean break of things which would allow those on the shop floor to get on with the job as the only way to school people in new tasks is to let them learn from their own mistakes.

Many times in my life I have been asked if I have thought all my work and efforts on behalf of the movement has been worth the trouble. Would I not have been better to have used it instead to improve my own personal position and used it to fulfill all sorts of so-called ambitions. Obviously situations cropped up where you could have taken advantage of them for your own personal ends, and there were many occasions when it would have been all too easy to have allowed considerations of a personal character to influence your actions. But sacrifice and principles are two important issues which cannot be effectively upheld without the other. So when I looked around on that evening of the presentation and heard and saw such genuine expressions of respect and even affection for my principles, work and integrity then I knew it had all been worthwhile.

Every department in the Sheepbridge complex had made a contribution or presentation and every factory in the Sheepbridge Combine had sent a delegation to make their own presentation. The union's president Hugh Scanlon gave me the AEU's award of merit for twenty-five years service — to be followed some years later by a special award for forty years — and all that was best in the labour and trade union movement had joined me to celebrate my retirement. It made me feel very humble and very proud and, of course, proved that principles and integrity are still the touchstones by which the labour movement judges its people.

Throughout a long life in the trade union and labour movement I have always maintained that the only way forward is to build a united labour movement to fight for a programme based on socialist policies. My own philosophy is based on the principles of Marxism and Leninism which, put simply, is that our present system of capitalism was developed, nurtured and kept in being for the purpose of exploiting the poor for the benefit of the rich. Whatever reforms that you may introduce to alleviate some of the harsher injustices you will never solve the internal contradiction between the necessity of a communal form of production with the private ownership of the means of production by the wealthy few. To make progress and enable mankind to take advantage of all the abundant wealth that can now be created there needs to be a change of the system to one whereby the means of production and distribution are socially owned and developed for the good of the majority.

My own personal activities have always been based on this basic understanding for without working for a complete change of system from capitalism to socialism all our efforts towards progress will founder. The labour movement, however, is made up of various strands and ideas and often it is necessary to build a unity of purpose around action to gain an immediate demand or to defend a particular position. I have always advocated this and it has enabled me to work with all sections of the movement around a variety of issues. I have also practised, and preached, to never become isolated from the main strain of the labour movement. I have my own point of view about the way the labour movement should develop and what socialism means and I shall continue to put forward such ideas and principles within the wider labour movement. I hope others will do the same but I will never allow sectarians from all sorts and all sides to declare I only belong to a sector. I was bred, reared and lived in the trade union and labour movement and I will always remain its representative.

It was therefore a very pleasant surprise when I was approached by the Chesterfield Borough Council's controlling Labour leader Bill Flanagan to accept the Freedom of the Borough. My attitude towards establishment honours is well known and usually my political views would have prevented me from accepting any such award. But when I considered the Freedom award it was something different. This was being offered by my own people and being offered because I had not compromised my principles, and to me it seemed a tribute to my own integrity. In the last hundred years the award — which is made to people of outstanding service to the town — has gone to just twenty-five people, all of whom were connected with either business or the council. To offer it to me was a complete break with tradition and by honouring me as a representative of the trade union and labour movement it recognised the contribution the labour movement had made to the well-being and interest of the majority of people in the town. If I had had any doubt, the fact that the Tories opposed the proposal put the seal on the honour and proved to me that my integrity was still intact.

Top: Dr. Stillman and I receiving the Freedom award from Chesterfield Mayor Ron Jepson in 1983 — and, below, a gold watch from my family; Front: Beryl, daughter Susan; Back: Grandaughter Nichola, grandaughter Dawn and daughters Janet, Mary and Kate.

I was very pleased and proud to be able to share the Freedom ceremony in November 1983 with Dr. Roger Stillman who used his knowledge and skills in the interest of the people. He was dedicated to the National Health Service and served it unswervingly over a long number of years. He earned the gratitude and respect of thousands of patients and earned the right and respect to be honoured as a man of medicine devoted to the people.

Men and women are social beings, all of us affected one way or another by the forces of the society in which we live and I believe real fulfilment for any person lies in service to fellow mankind. There is much talk these days of what is wrong with society, of the evils of permissiveness and moral laxity in the narrowest sense. But I do not think these are the real problems. However, it does involve morality, ethics and our concept of human values and our challenge is to root out anything and everything that distorts human relationship.

This is best expressed and illustrated in the widespread and implicit acceptance of the concept and term of the rat race. It conjures up a picture where we are scurrying around, scrambling for positions, trampling on others, back stabbling — all in pursuit of personal success. I have always rejected the attitudes, values and false morality that underlie these actions. The rat race is for rats. We are not rats, we are human beings with feelings of care, compassion and human dignity. We should, therefore, reject the insidious pressures in society that would blunt our critical faculties to all that is happening around us that would caution silence in face of injustice lest we jeopardise our chances of promotion of self-advancement. Otherwise before you know where you are, you are a fully paid up member of the rat pack.

The family with hugh Scanlon, former AEU President, at my retirement ceremony in 1975.

For me the price was far too high. But following such a philosophy can sometimes be both a daunting and lonely path where survival largely depends on those around you. Without the help and support of my family I could have achieved nothing. I was both proud and privileged to receive the Freedom of the Borough of Chesterfield but at least half of the award belongs to my wife, Beryl, who has been a tower of strength when circumstances dictated it, but who has equally been prepared to puncture any balloons of pomposity that may have been floated as a result of undue enthusiasms or rare praise.

In to the 21st century: Chesterfield Trades Council's latest banner depicts the modern worker and the main areas of employment in the town today: the health service, engineering, packaging and mining, with the central figure reaching out to the future.